# THE READING TRIANGLE

**PARENTS ▲ TEACHER ▲ CHILD**

YOU *CAN* HELP YOUR CHILD LEARN TO READ

Linda M. Clinard

*Illustrated by Duane Bibby*

**DAVID S. LAKE PUBLISHERS**
Belmont, California

Cover photo: Karen Stafford Rantzman



ISBN-0-8224-5815-2

Library of Congress Catalog Card Number: 84-62866

Printed in the United States of America

1. 9 8 7 6 5 4 3 2 1

a Metcalf

# THE READING TRIANGLE

**PARENTS ▴ TEACHER ▴ CHILD**

# Table of Contents


To the Reader .......... vii

Introduction .......... 1

## Section One: The Language Triangle

Part One: GAINING INFORMATION .......... 7

Chapter 1: Listening .......... 9
- Listening: An Infant or Young Child .......... 10
- Listening: The Older Child .......... 13

Chapter 2: Reading .......... 17
- Four Keys to Reading Success .......... 17
- The Need to Read .......... 18
- First Encounters with Reading .......... 18
- Handling Books .......... 19
- Reading with Children .......... 21
- Reading Around Home .......... 22
- Influences on Reading Success .......... 24
- Deeper into Reading .......... 27

Summary: Gaining Information .......... 31

Part Two: UNDERSTANDING .......... 33

Chapter 3: Thinking on Our Own .......... 35
- Depending on Someone .......... 35
- Figuring Out Meaning on Our Own .......... 37

Chapter 4: Time to Think .......... 41
- Allow Time .......... 41
- Take Time .......... 42

Chapter 5: Getting Involved .......... 43
- Actively Participate .......... 43
- Guided Involvement .......... 44

Summary: Understanding .......... 45

Part Three: COMMUNICATING .......... 47

Chapter 6: What We Say .......... 49
- An Infant or Young Child .......... 49
- The Older Child .......... 51

Chapter 7: What We Do .......... 53
- Signals Children Send .......... 53
- Drawing and Writing .......... 55

Summary: Communicating .......... 61

Summary: Section One .......... 63

## Section Two: Putting the Reading Triangle to Work

Introduction .......... 67

Part One: GUIDELINES FOR COMMUNICATION .......... 68

Part Two: THE READING LOG .......... 73

Part Three: READING OBSERVATIONS AND ACTIVITIES .......... 75

- Attitude, Incentive, Behavior .......... 77
- Organization .......... 81
- The Alphabet .......... 85
- Word Recognition .......... 91
- Word Meaning .......... 97
- Comprehension .......... 101
- Oral Reading/Silent Reading .......... 104
- Writing and Drawing .......... 108

Summary: Section Two .......... 111

Some Closing Thoughts .......... 112

Further Information and Ideas for Parents .......... 113

Reading Glossary .......... 117

Index .......... 121

# To the Reader

THE SUGGESTIONS and examples offered in this book are based upon the author's experience in the field of reading education, and are believed to apply to most individual characteristics likely to be encountered by parents and teachers in the field of reading education. However, as every case is individual, and unique problems beyond those discussed in this book may exist, there is no guarantee that this book alone can fill every individual's needs. Accordingly, the author suggests that it is always wise for the parent to consult with teachers, reading specialists, pediatricians, and other professionals as the child's individual needs may warrant. Indeed, *The Reading Triangle* is intended above all to provide a "working knowledge" of the reading process, so that you, the parent, can help your child more effectively on your own, and also, so that you can better communicate with teachers and other professionals personally involved in helping your child learn. Only by comfortable and effective communication can you be sure that your child is receiving the full benefit of the reading triangle—a relationship comprised of parent, teacher, and child working together.

# Introduction

WHEN I MET Mrs. Kane, the mother of two preschoolers, at a friend's home recently, she turned to me looking as though she were begging for a logical answer:

"Do you realize how confusing it is to be a parent who wants to do everything possible to help a child read? Some teachers and parents are telling me not to worry. My two children will learn all they need in order to read successfully when they get to school. I am told not to spend money or much time in seeing that they begin to read early. On the other hand, I am being urged by others to follow a specific plan and buy materials to prepare my children at home. What should I do?"

I explained that first we must realize that reading cannot be isolated from the rest of a child's language experiences. If we emphasize learning words in print before a child has had opportunities to experience language in other ways, all the reading practice in the world will go to waste.

Mrs. Kane leaned toward me and still appeared skeptical as she responded, "That sounds nice but WHAT DO YOU MEAN?" I used a small piece of paper on a notepad to illustrate how reading is related to a child's total language development.

I explained that reading is part of a broader picture of what I call "The Language Triangle".

*The Language Triangle*

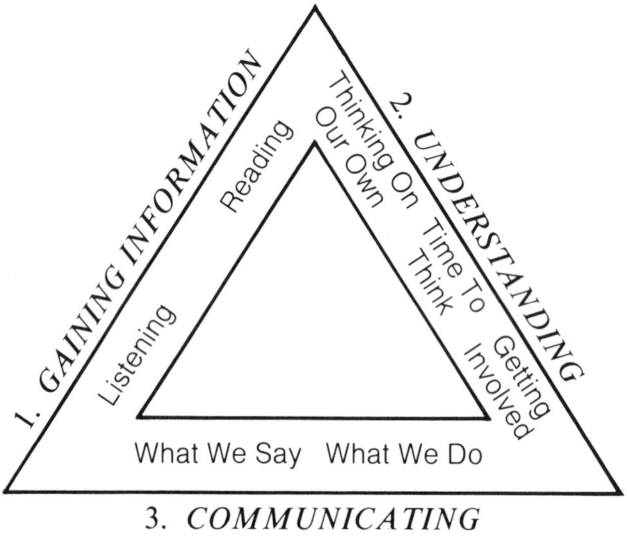


I use the triangle to show three important processes of language: (1) gaining information, (2) understanding, and (3) communicating. I showed Mrs. Kane how I place these three areas of language within a triangle to emphasize that they are related. They are not isolated processes which develop by themselves. Each part of the triangle depends on the other if all areas of language are to grow. The Language Triangle should include experiences in:

1. GAINING INFORMATION by *listening* and *reading*.
2. UNDERSTANDING what has been heard and read. First we depend on someone to help us understand a new experience. Eventually, we need to *think more on our own*. Whether we are depending on someone or thinking on our own, we need *time to think*. We also need to *get involved* in what we are to learn.
3. COMMUNICATING our understanding by *what we say and do*.

Mrs. Kane said that this triangular picture of how reading is a part of language was helpful, but she needed some practical ideas. I asked her to tell me a little about each of her youngsters. As she did, I shared some of the ideas which are presented in the rest of this book. Mrs. Kane and I have remained in touch over the months, and she has been able to let me know what works best, as many other parents and teachers have done over the years.

I have developed a firm belief through such encounters that many parents want to better understand how reading is related to their child's total language development. My intentions are to show this reading and language relationship in as relevant a way as possible. Thus, interested parents may help their children develop in their learning and enjoyment of reading to the fullest.

I have prepared this book in two sections. In Section One, I share information and experiences related to the three areas of The Language Triangle: (1) Gaining Information, (2) Understanding, and (3) Communicating. Section Two offers parents, children, and teachers guidelines for observing and identifying strengths and needs in reading and other language areas. Suggestions based on those strengths and needs are given to help children grow in reading.

Although many of the ideas in Section One appear to relate to the early development of a child's learning experience, I believe it is never too late to learn. I have tried to illustrate this belief by sharing experiences which I have had in teaching older children. I have worked with many older children who may have missed early language experiences, but who were helped dramatically when the principles of The Language Triangle were better understood and applied by parent, child, and teacher (The Reading Triangle).

Therefore, the suggestions which I offer throughout this book are intended to serve as a guide in providing children with successful reading and language experiences, whether they are just beginning the adventure into hearing and using language or have been engaged in it for several years.

# SECTION ONE

## THE LANGUAGE TRIANGLE

# Part One

## GAINING INFORMATION

THE FIRST PHASE of The Language Triangle involves (1) GAINING INFORMATION.

It is fun and exciting to experience new things each day. Children can GAIN INFORMATION about new experiences primarily by *listening* and *reading*.

# 1

# LISTENING

*The Language Triangle*

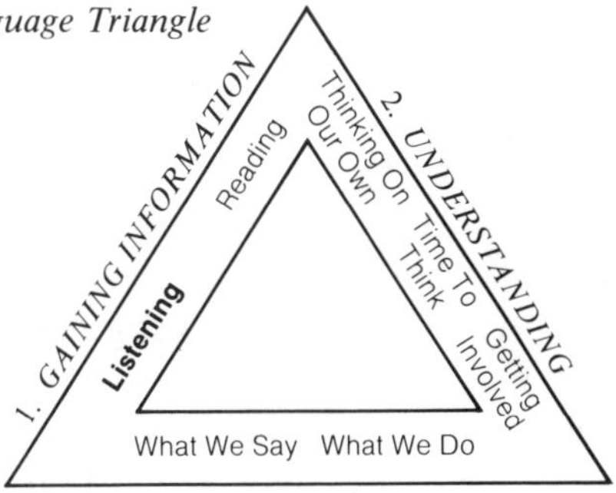


WE USUALLY begin gaining information through LISTENING. A healthy baby is introduced to this world of sounds and words even before birth by listening, and listening becomes the way we gain new information most often throughout our lives.

Jane, a friend of mine who was expecting her first child, told me recently that she was concerned about giving her child a good start in reading. She asked, "How can I be sure I am doing the right thing from the day the baby is born?" I am finding that more and more mothers of infants and very young children are asking similar questions, and I'm excited when I can talk with those who are eager to start that early. As I told Jane, and have shared with other parents like her, the best preparation for reading comes by helping our children understand what they hear even before they are born!

We feel awkward if someone catches us talking enthusiastically to our newborn baby or lovingly speaking to the child we feel moving even before the baby is born. But we need to lose our inhibitions! Children need to hear us and hear other sounds around them. As they begin to understand what these sounds, words, and sentences mean, they will be better prepared to interpret printed words later.

I believe that from the very beginning WE NEED TO TAKE THE LEAD IN HELPING A CHILD HEAR AND UNDERSTAND WHAT LANGUAGE IS ALL ABOUT — not by just the words we say, but by the way we say them and by the types of experiences we offer as we speak. Your child will remember and understand a great deal more about what is heard if the experience involves more than just listening. Whenever possible, encourage your child to see, touch, smell, taste as you explain what is being experienced.

## LISTENING: AN INFANT OR YOUNG CHILD

I remember stopping at my friend Mary's home recently to copy a recipe. Her son, Joe, who was five months old at the time, was sitting in his high chair while his mother was ironing. I noticed that Joe occasionally looked toward me and then back to the ironing and his mother. He watched the iron go back and forth. If he turned away, he looked quickly back to the iron when his mother turned it causing it to make a hissing sound as steam escaped.

After I finished copying the recipe, Mary and I sat on the floor around the coffee table. She placed Joe near us on the floor. Immediately, the telephone rang. The baby looked at the telephone or in that general direction. He watched as his mother answered it. While she was gone, I enjoyed my own conversation with Joe. When Mary rejoined us, we were able to settle down with a cup of tea to catch up on the latest news.

I had noticed that Joe looked at us as we talked and then turned to other objects which were moving outside. It was a windy day, and he could see the trees swaying and paper blowing on the neighbor's back step.

Our conversation turned to the subject of reading, as it usually does when I'm around — and I must admit that it's my favorite topic of conversation. Mary said she and her husband were talking recently about whether they would send Joe to nursery school, so he could get an early start in reading. She had promised her husband to ask my opinion as to what they could be doing at home to prepare Joe. They wanted to do whatever was necessary to get him ready to read, regardless of their decision on enrolling him in an early reading program.

I began by explaining how reading cannot be separated from the rest of Joe's language development, that she needed to start by giving him opportunities to hear and understand the words he hears before he ever sees them in print. I used examples of what had been happening in the few minutes since I had been visiting that day.

I related to Mary my observations that, as she was ironing, Joe was looking at the iron going back and forth and was especially attentive when he heard the hissing sound that the steam would make.

Had she realized how important it was to bring Joe into a conversation about the iron and what was happening? For example, she could tell him that she was using the iron on daddy's shirt and that she was going back and forth with the iron. When the steam would hiss, she could explain and show by her actions that it was HOT steam. Many mothers of very young children, especially infants, respond when I make such suggestions by saying, "But they don't really understand what you are saying."

Mary didn't respond that way. She grasped the ideas and said, "Well, when the phone rang, I should have told him that I was going to answer the TELEPHONE." Exactly! I went on to suggest that she speak in short sentences, always emphasizing the specific words which were most important in the sentence. If she noticed Joe looking outside at the swaying trees, she could say, "See the TREES swaying." Once he seemed to understand *trees*, she could begin emphasizing more words in the sentence.

A child needs to participate meaningfully in a language environment. Your child is hearing and seeing things, and at the beginning our children need help to understand what has been seen and heard. We should never assume that a child is not understanding and then give up. A friend who is a speech and language teacher once told me, "If you are in the same room with your youngster for more than a few minutes and have not spoken, you have lost a valuable opportunity to interact in ways which will pay off later."

It is important to note that in Joe's case, I did not suggest that Mary tell her son *everything* that was in the room. She should only tune in to those things which were important to the situation, particularly those in which Joe showed an interest. If she tried to explain too much which was not important, Joe would not have a reason for remembering the particular words or ideas the next time a similar situation occurred.

Some children will show more attention to sounds or objects than others. Just because a youngster is not looking intently at something should not be a reason for remaining silent. We need to converse and encourage children to participate in what is happening so a child will eventually develop an interest. When we are filling the tub with water, watching a car pass on the street, or listening to an airplane pass overhead, we need to actively describe . . . name . . . use expression . . .!

I also shared with Mary that we can provide important listening experiences when we aren't speaking with our children. Record players and tape recorders are important tools. I told Mary that I would never forget a three year old boy asking me, "Do you know how to say SUPER-CALI-FRAGIL-ISTIC-EXPI-ALI-DOCIOUS?" Before I had a chance to respond, the boy's mother quickly inserted, "He learned that in just a few days after we bought the record after seeing Mary Poppins." Children need to hear music with varying rhythm patterns (classical, popular, children's songs, etc.), nursery rhymes, stories, poems . . . Children love to have others dance and sing with them. They will see how to respond to what is heard on records or tapes. It is also great to put a record or tape on to play as you put your little one to bed. This is especially nice if the machine automatically shuts off. Your child can slumber off listening to a favorite story, song, poem . . . I am *not* suggesting that the record players or tape recorders take your place! Records and tapes are good ways of *adding* to what you personally share by talking and singing to your child.

## LISTENING: THE OLDER CHILD

Jerry, an 11-year-old fifth grader, was new to our school. He had been through a number of years in a special reading class and had repeated second grade. In spite of these efforts, he was still one to two years behind in reading. His parents, his teacher (Mr. Reynolds), and Jerry met with me to discuss what we could offer at our school.

When I first met Jerry, I remember he appeared to be a very quiet boy who spoke in soft, short sentences. I asked him to bring a sample of his reading work to our conference. He brought his reading workbook. On one page, he had been asked to write *sh, ch, th*, or *ph* at the beginning or end of words which were to match pictures on the page.

Under the picture of a *ship*, he had written a *b*. Under a *chain*, he had written an *r*. Nothing had been written under the picture of a *thimble*. He wrote *p* under the *graph*. I asked him to tell me the names of the pictures. For the *ship*, he said "boat." For the *chain*, he said "rope." When he saw the picture of the *thimble*, he said, "I'm not sure what it's called." He went on to say, "I know what you use it for. My mom uses it when she sews, but I'm not sure what you call it." When I had him point to the *graph*, he called it a "map." Even though he knew that he was supposed to place a *ch, sh, th*, or *ph* under the pictures, he had difficulty thinking of words which would represent the pictures and have those letter-sounds. These letter-sound combinations are called *digraphs*.

It wasn't the digraphs which were causing Jerry difficulty, but he was having trouble thinking of the names of the pictures which would contain those sounds. I needed to explore whether it was a problem of not remembering words to which he had been exposed frequently, or were there other reasons for his difficulties? There is rarely an easy answer to such a question, but further discussion helped us know where to start. Jerry's parents revealed that Jerry seemed to have a good memory for meaningful and interesting things which he heard or saw each day. They did admit, however, that they had assumed that he knew what to call simple, everyday objects. They had not consciously bothered to check to see how much he understood. This gave us the necessary clues for beginning to help Jerry. He appeared to need language understanding, not phonics. Jerry did not appear to have had a rich background of listening experience at home. In investigating further, I found that whenever Jerry needed to use words in writing sentences or in sharing ideas with the class, he rarely varied his pattern of sentences. The sentences would be short and almost seem repetitive. "I like to play ball. I like to listen to good records. I like to help my father."

Jerry needed to know that he did not appear to have significant problems with letter-sounds. Rather, we needed to begin by *emphasizing and strengthening Jerry's understanding of words.* He should be encouraged to think about the meanings of words and sentences. Jerry needed to determine meanings by the way words are used or where and how they are used. BUT he required more than we could do at school. He needed to use the new information as he learned about things around his home, too. Jerry needed to be encouraged to listen carefully and participate in discussions.

He would benefit from experience in using new words and ideas whenever possible. As he sharpened his ability to listen and speak, he would be better equipped to interpret what he read.

If Jerry failed to show signs of improvement once some of these suggestions had been tried for a month or two, or if he became frustrated when asked to listen more, we would need to look into having his hearing more thoroughly tested. He had passed all the hearing screenings offered at school and during regular pediatric examinations, but more specialized testing might be necessary. We would consult the speech and language pathologist in our school if such a hearing evaluation were necessary. Whether the more specialized testing proved necessary or not, we still planned to consult with the speech and language teacher for further ideas on helping Jerry improve in his understanding of language.

As Jerry had opportunities to hear and use words, he began to improve. His family became very creative when thinking of ways to help him. The most consistent activity which led to success involved *reading to him*. Somehow his parents had thought an eleven-year-old boy would not want to be read to, but Mr. Reynolds read to his fifth grade class regularly. He told Jerry's parents that even though the books he read were difficult, there was always a race to the library for the book when he finished reading it. Once students had heard the stories, they were more excited about the stories and could better understand them when reading on their own.

If Jerry needed to write a report and had difficulty reading the encyclopedia, his parents were no longer hesitant to read the information to him. They would ask him to tell them in his own words what had been read. Once he had the ideas, he was better prepared to write a report using the information. He would often then try to read the encyclopedia himself. Hearing the information and new words first helped him become familiar with what he could put into his own words and eventually write.

You may be saying, "I'm glad you found out how to help Jerry, but that's not what my child needs." Every child *is* different, but we can't use that fact as a means of telling ourselves that our child is so unique that — "None of these suggestions about listening apply to my situation." Whether or not your child has begun to succeed in his reading venture, I hope we can agree that all children need to listen and understand what they hear if they are to understand what they read.

# 2

# READING

The Language Triangle

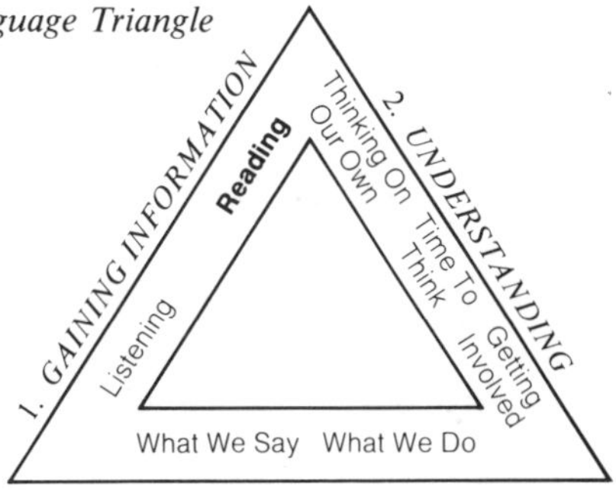


MANY PARENTS and teachers have brought children to me proudly exclaiming, "This child can really read!" As I listen to and watch these children, I find that each one approaches words and stories differently. Are they reading? YES — but each child may be unlocking only certain doors on the way to successful reading experiences.

**FOUR KEYS TO READING SUCCESS**

I believe there are four keys to reading success. Successful readers approach printed material with (1) **P**urpose, (2) **U**nderstanding, (3) good **R**ecall, and (4) **E**njoyment — **PURE** Reading.

No one key can lead to success by itself. Some children have purposes or good intentions, but *noble purposes alone do not improve reading*. For example, your child may be reading for the *purpose* of saying words correctly. If a child doesn't *understand* and *recall* what is said, however, very important keys are missing. Even when a child has a good memory and can recall most of what is seen and heard, reading will not improve unless one understands. Your child may have purpose, understanding, and good recall, but *enjoyment* is essential. When children enjoy what is read, they will read more. One of the best ways to improve in anything is to practice. When we enjoy something, we don't resist practicing as much. This is as true in learning to read as it is in any other part of our life. Thus, THE FOUR KEYS THAT LEAD TO READING SUCCESS CANNOT BE ISOLATED FROM ONE ANOTHER. They are all essential.

Since each of the four keys to reading are so closely related, I will share thoughts and experiences in the remainder of this chapter which are intended to provide you with insight, information, and ideas that will lead your child into using ALL FOUR KEYS. I do not develop each "key" separately. I don't believe it is possible to say, "This is how to develop (1) Purpose, then (2) Understanding, (3) Recall, and (4) Enjoyment."

Each idea should do more than help with one key at a time. So I do believe that if you understand and apply the ideas I share, you can help your child develop PURE reading to its fullest.

**THE NEED TO READ**

Children must see that reading is all around us and is necessary for success and survival. The only way children will sense the need to read is by seeing those around them reading. I'm not just speaking about reading books and newspapers. You need to read aloud from the prescription bottles as you give your child medicine. Read the street signs out loud as you drive. Read the names of restaurants and stores as you enter them with your child. We can't assume that our children will see the need to read unless they know we are reading. We need to set an example. Children will rapidly begin to appreciate that reading has many purposes. You will be amazed at how they will understand, recall, and enjoy these experiences with reading.

**FIRST ENCOUNTERS WITH READING**

The most common first encounter with words in print comes in seeing them on the objects they represent. For example, children will see the labels on cereal boxes; names of stores and restaurants on the buildings; brand names on food, shampoos, medicine bottles;

titles of favorite programs on a T.V. screen. Words are everywhere.

When *meaningful surroundings* offer the major clues for recognizing and understanding words, this is one form of *reading in context*. Thus, very young children are taking their first steps toward reading on their own by using meaningful surroundings or "context" to help them recognize words.

I remember a mother telling me about her two-year-old daughter who could *read* the word McDonald's whether she saw it on the restaurant or in an ad. I was skeptical until one day we were in a car together riding down a busy street, and I heard this child shout, "EK-DONELS." When I looked behind us, I saw that, indeed, we had just passed a McDonald's restaurant. The word was in large letters on the front of the building. A few minutes later, we passed another restaurant where the word was printed on the "golden arches." Sure enough, the child said, "EK-DONELS." When I printed the word on paper in large letters, she did not recognize it, but when I drew some "golden arches" behind the word, she read it. She relied on some meaningful clue or symbol to trigger her recognition of the word.

A few months later, when I was visiting this two-year-old, I thought I would try a little experiment. I wrote the word on a blank sheet of paper again, and this time she read it correctly — without any context clues. She had needed the clues at first, but now she was recognizing it by itself. What was even more important than this two-year-old's ability to read the word, was her confidence in answering my question, "What do you do at McDonald's?" She replied, "Eat num-num ham-bers." She understood the meaning behind the word — and was demonstrating early signs of PURE reading!

## HANDLING BOOKS

Another important step that will lead to PURE reading comes with handling books. I spoke recently with a mother who said she was afraid to allow her three-year-old to handle a book for fear of his tearing it to shreds. I will admit that such fears may be well founded, especially if a child has not had experience in handling any types of books and if the child has been difficult to manage.

I have seen situations, however, in which children have been taught to handle books carefully before the age of three. The important thing was that the child had seen others handle books with respect. Then the child was gradually introduced to handling books independently.

I have a friend who read to her child from the time she brought him home from the hospital. At about three months of age, she gave him books with cardboard or non-toxic cloth pages. He would attempt to flip the pages back and forth. Within a few months, she noticed he was making an effort to see what was on individual pages, not randomly flipping the pages. Sometimes he became frustrated because he could not turn the pages easily, so she clipped clothespins to each page. He used the pins as handles and could turn the pages more easily. His frustration ceased and his enjoyment again increased. By the time her little boy was a year old, he had pulled the clothespins off and was turning the pages without difficulty. He didn't turn them in sequence, but he had the idea.

In order to give him opportunities to handle books with paper pages, he was first given magazines with interesting pictures. He had seen his mother and father turn the pages, but he still needed to be watched to see if he knew what to do. He needed to practice when it wouldn't matter if pages were torn. His mother or father would look through the magazine with him, helping him turn pages. They praised him when he found a picture he liked by turning a page without tearing or badly wrinkling it. If a page was torn, he could see what would happen if he hurried or became too rough. This youngster was able to turn pages in a magazine before he was two, but some children, because of their personality and enthusiasm, might not be able to succeed in this until later. This requires time and practice — AND it must be done with interesting magazines. Remember . . . reading should be for *enjoyment, as well as for learning.*

Eventually, a child can be given a favorite book which contains paper pages with the supervision of someone who can watch and help. If a child tears a page in a good book, the cardboard or cloth books may be used more often, along with more practice on the magazines. Children learn through experience that rough treatment has its consequences.

## READING WITH CHILDREN

One of the best ways to introduce reading to children is to read WITH them. If you share books that are interesting, your child will learn a great deal. I would offer one caution, however, since hearing about five-year-old Laura.

**Setting An Example**: Laura could read practically any book she was given — BUT she could read only if the book were held upside down! A look into her background revealed that Laura's parents read regularly to her at bedtime. When Laura was asked why she held the books upside down, she said, "That's how I got used to it when Mom and Daddy read to me." It was found that Laura's parents would put her to bed and sat facing her with the book in their laps as they read. When they would finish reading a page, they held the book up so Laura could see the pictures. As they read, Laura had begun to look at the words without their realizing she was doing so. She taught herself to read from right-to-left and upside down! When this unique style of reading was discovered in kindergarten, Laura's parents and teacher feared that she had a severe learning problem. She didn't. She had developed her method of reading because that was the way she had been seeing the words as books were read to her at bedtime.

After some careful help and guidance, Laura, her parents, and teacher were able to view her need realistically. Laura needed to see that words and sentences are read from left-to-right in our culture. After a few months of careful guidance, Laura began to turn things around.

Thus, we should have a child sit on our lap or next to us. If that isn't possible, we need to hold the book up so the child can correctly see the pictures and words as we read.

We are setting an example by showing how pages are turned. The child can also see that a book has a beginning and ending.

As we run our hands under the words and gesture to the pictures they describe, children will begin seeing that the words describe pictures and objects.

**Get Your Child Involved:** You can get your very young child involved as you read a favorite story.

I have always enjoyed listening and watching as my husband reads to our daughter Anne. I love to hear her reaction as her dad reads a familiar story and either leaves off a word or phrase at the end of a sentence or changes the ending. At first, before she could say the words he had left out or correct the ones he had changed, she would still react. She would either point repeatedly to the page as though she were telling him to "Say it again — and correctly this time." Or she might point to the picture which illustrated the correct word. This happened more as she grew older. She loved participating! We loved seeing how well she understood. Eventually, as Anne began to talk more, she welcomed the chance to "fill in." We would read, "The big bad wolf told the little pig . . ." Anne would finish, "Little pig, little pig let me come in." As she grew more familiar with the story, she would go on to complete the whole page or the entire story in words she recalled our reading to her.

**Memorizing And Using Meaning**: As children adopt a favorite book, they will often memorize the story and may make up words which they think should be describing the pictures on a given page. Such first attempts at reading in books should *not* be discouraged. Knowing words from memory and recognizing that words should fit the meaning of the pictures on a page are important tools for future reading success. Children will eventually develop other abilities which will help them become well-rounded readers, but these first efforts should be praised because the child is excited about reading. Such enjoyment must be encouraged!

## READING AROUND HOME

Usually by age five or six (and before that for some children), you may want to do more with reading around home. Here are two ideas which take your children into experiences with words around the house and elsewhere.

**Around The House**: Your child may choose interesting objects around the house. Have your child describe the object or tell what it does as you write the description on a strip of paper. Important words may be colored or underlined. Place the strip near or on the object it describes.

Be creative in adding to this idea, but use discretion. Start a room at a time with a few objects at a time. Don't overwhelm the child, and don't clutter up your home with strips of paper. Just remember to have your child involved in choosing the objects. This will make learning to read more interesting and enjoyable.

Occasionally take the sentence strips off the objects, mix them up a few at a time. See which ones the child can read and place on the correct object. As a phrase is learned, put it in an "I Can Read" box for periodic review. Have your child place them on the object again, and together you may decide to leave a few of them out to review.

**Language Experience Stories**: There is another natural way to give your child meaningful experiences with reading by showing how what is thought and spoken can be written and read.

At a very early age, when children are not yet speaking in complete sentences, they love to draw. Most young toddlers draw for the fun of it. They are not trying to draw something specific at first. When your two or three year old begins to name what has been drawn, you should get involved in helping your child "see the words" that are being said. You may not recognize the "doggie" or "monster" in the picture, but don't let that stop you. *Write what your child says it is*. A very young child will begin to see that spoken words can be made into written words that stand for something meaningful.

You can help your child continue to see the relationship between what is said and what can be written and then read as you enjoy going to new places and share new experiences together. Encourage your child to talk about new experiences, or even old ones. Your child can capture the memories of what has been enjoyed by drawing or collecting pictures. Ask your child to tell you about the experience illustrated by the pictures. Encourage your child to watch as you write the description. You are helping your child see

Lang. Exp.
see also Chapter 7

how words that are thought and spoken can be written and read. This provides important insights into how stories in books are created.

This is one form of what has been called the "Language Experience Approach" to reading. The Language Experience Approach offers a way to guide your child in applying a knowledge of speaking, thinking, reading, drawing, and writing. (See the end of Chapter Seven for further information about this approach.)

## INFLUENCES ON READING SUCCESS

Children should be introduced naturally to reading by the time they are six or seven, using some of the ideas offered earlier in this chapter. Now I would like to share information which I hope will provide insight as we continue to guide our children toward reading success.

Once children enter school, it is not long before parents and teachers are filled with questions, "Why is Jason succeeding so well while Jeff is not? They are both being given the same opportunities." It may look as though they are being offered similar opportunities, but there is more to consider.

Regardless of the age or background of each child, I have learned to listen and look for clues which guide me in knowing what may be influencing each child's success. I talk with the child, parents, and the teacher to explore four areas which influence all of learning — especially language and reading: (1) Physical Characteristics; (2) Attitude and Behavior; (3) Home and Social Environment; and (4) Educational Background.

**Physical Characteristics**: Is there any physical reason why the child is having difficulty? A variety of physical characteristics will influence learning, but hearing and vision are most closely related to reading and language development.

Children who have ear problems (fluid build-up, frequent infections, severe or chronic allergies . . . ) are often frustrated with various language and reading-related tasks. They will become frustrated or agitated when asked to sit still to listen to a story. They may have difficulty telling the difference among letters and the sounds they represent while reading and spelling. Good hearing is vital if a child is to succeed in speaking, reading, and spelling!

Good vision is also a must for successful reading. I'm sure you may be saying, "Well, I would think so!" You would be amazed at the number of children who are frustrated with reading because vision difficulties have not been thoroughly identified. I have noticed that many vision problems related to reading frustration are not identified until third or fourth grade (9 or 10 years of age). In first and second grades, the stories are short and the print is large. The print gets much smaller as the sentences get longer and closer together in third grade and above.

Do you notice your child getting tired easily when reading? Does your child read a little at a time and then look away? We often think a child is being stubborn when refusing to complete an assignment, but these and other signs of discomfort may be telling you there may be a vision problem — not a specific reading difficulty.

When your child is having persistent problems in reading and language-related areas, I strongly recommend a thorough physical examination, including vision and hearing *testing*. Vision and hearing *screenings* as offered by the school and the pediatrician may not be enough. Be sure your child has no physical barriers that will hinder success.

**Attitude And Behavior**: What is your child *telling* you through attitudes and behaviors? I look for signals a child may be sending without saying a word. Section Two of this book offers a list of

p. 77 →

specific attitude and behavior observations. The observations are followed by suggestions for improvement.

Your child may have a negative attitude toward reading — or may want to read, but certain behaviors may appear to be hindering progress. We often need to begin by improving the attitude or managing the behavior, rather than drilling on reading activities.

**Home And Social Environment**: Family members and friends have attitudes and habits related to speaking and reading which strongly influence a child. How we speak and read will be reflected in our children.

Two of the most common questions parents ask me about reading at home are: (1) What can I do to help our child with reading at home without becoming a tutor? and (2) Just how does T.V. affect my child's reading? Is it good or bad?

***Taking time out for reading*** is the best, most *non-tutoring* thing you can do to improve reading at home. Use that time to set an example for your children. This "time-out" should be a relaxed time which fits naturally into the family schedule. It can be the same time each day, but in most homes that just isn't possible.

If things work best in your home by setting a routine, then have a "family time-out for reading" just before or after dinner — or just before the children go to bed.

If a regular schedule doesn't work in your home, set a goal of reading with your children at least three to four times a week. It's often hard to remember in a busy schedule whether or not you have taken sufficient time to read with your children each week. Start marking your calendar! Set tentative times, make the time available for reading, then mark it off when you do take the time. It is so important!

During your time-outs, there will be days when you and your children choose to read silently — books, newspapers, magazines . . . Encourage your children to tell you about what they read. On other days, you may read something to your children — something they want to hear. There should be frequent times when your children share stories, plays, or letters from friends or relatives with you. Make reading aloud a sharing time — not a drilling of reading and word recognition skills. Remember that if your child wants to read something that is too difficult and frustration seems to set in, you can read that to your child first. Once children hear a story, they are better equipped to read it on their own later.

After reading this, you may have good intentions for having a "time-out for reading." Don't just intend — PLEASE TAKE THE TIME TO DO IT!

***Television can influence your child's reading*** — positively or negatively. Does your child sit quietly and stare without saying a word while watching a program or even afterward? If so, your child may be gaining new information and new ideas, but you have no way of knowing what has been understood because there is no communication. We will continue wondering how positively or negatively our children have been influenced by television unless we (1) are selective in what our children are to watch, (2) watch television as much as we can with our children to know what they are seeing and hearing, (3) talk about the programs with our children, and (4) encourage our children to tell us (or watch for signals that show us) what they learned.

Television can get children excited about reading. It can introduce them to ideas or concepts you don't have time to introduce. T.V. is also a great motivator in that children get excited about reading the stories they see dramatized in television programs and movies.

I do not believe that parents should become "tutors," but there is no way to deny the vital role of family and friends in (1) setting an example and (2) helping a child practice and apply what is learned in school.

**Educational Background**: This is the fourth area which influences a child's success in learning to read. I look at what a child knows and how that knowledge is applied. To what extent has the child been guided in finding the keys to reading success — Purpose, Understanding, Recall, and Enjoyment?

## DEEPER INTO READING

What happens when there is a question about a student's reading progress? I ask the student to read something which has not been seen before but which should be easy to read. If the student has difficulty, I look more deeply into why frustration may be encountered while attempting to read. I begin by exploring the four areas which influence learning: (1) physical characteristics, (2) attitude and behavior, (3) home and social environment, and (4) educational background. Then I examine specific reading areas on the basis of what I heard and saw when the child talked with me and read to me.

Let me share two of the specific areas I examine: (1) Word Recognition and (2) Word Meaning. I look at other areas, as you will see in Section Two, but let me begin with these.

**Word Recognition**: We need to look at the way our children approach new words. Readers tend to rely on one or a combination of three ways to read words: (a) Context, (b) Memory, and (c) Letter-Sounds or Word-Parts.

***Context***: Remember that young children usually first learn to read new words by getting clues from meaningful surroundings. They first recognize words which they see on familiar objects: cereal boxes, candy bars, favorite restaurants . . . Do you recall the little two-year-old girl who showed me she could read "EK-DONELS" (McDonald's)? Eventually children recognize words because they fit the meaning expressed in a picture. Then when reading stories, children can tell that the words *make sense* or fit the meaningful "context" of sentences within the stories.

***Memory***: A second way your child will recognize a word will be through memory. Children recall what they have seen or heard before. At first, your child may appear to be memorizing words and sentences from favorite stories, but few children are actually looking at or distinguishing the individual words within the sentences. In most cases they are using the pictures as clues (context), and then repeating what someone has taken the time to read to them. Even though many children are relying mostly on picture clues at this point, they are beginning to exercise an important tool necessary for reading — memory.

With your guidance and example as you read more stories together, your child will eventually look at the individual words and watch how they flow together to form sentences. Children differ widely in the degree to which they are able to recall the words they see. As your child reads more, words will be encountered which grow longer and harder to remember. Thus, children won't be able to rely totally on memorizing words. It will get too frustrating. They will need to use "context" and "letter-sounds" or "word-parts" to unlock words which cannot be memorized.

There will always be certain words which need to be memorized. Such words are often referred to as "sight words" or "high-frequency words." Sight words do not usually have a letter-sound pattern nor can they be easily recognized from the context of the sentence. Sight words can be remembered by associating them with other, similar-looking words or by just recalling their general shape or configuration.

***Letter-Sounds And Word-Parts***: The third way most children learn to recognize new words is through the use of letter-sounds or word-parts. This has often been referred to as "sounding-out."

*Phonics* is one term used by many with regard to the letter-sound approach. *Linguistics* is another term closely related to the teaching of words through sounds and letter-patterns. *Structural Analysis* refers to unlocking longer words through the use of word-parts such as syllables, prefixes, suffixes . . . The methods and philosophies behind these approaches may differ, but we don't have time to discuss the differences here. It is important to recognize that the use of letter-sounds and word-parts are ways of helping individuals read new words.

Few children before the age of five or six figure out on their own that letters represent sounds which may be blended to form words. Even when letter-sound relationships have been taught as early as 3 or 4 years of age, the majority of children will not fully understand and apply sound-blending on their own until after five or six. Just as children are growing physically, they are maturing intellectually. There are certain types of relationships that take time and experience to understand and apply. Such is the case when we expect a child to grasp how a letter *stands for* one or more sounds. Thus, I believe that knowledge of letter-sounds and word-parts can be helpful in unlocking new words, but we should not emphasize this approach until children are ready to understand and apply what they are presented. They must also be encouraged to balance this letter-sound approach with the use of context and memory.

You can see how children need to adapt the use of all three word-recognition techniques. Since each child is unique, I cannot predict how your child will first read a word. I do believe, however, that parents, teachers, and children need to be aware of the three ways words are most often recognized: Context, Memory, and Letter-Sounds or Word-Parts.

If you understand and agree with what I have just shared, you will no longer be numbered among those who are constantly telling a child, "JUST SOUND-IT-OUT." Try instead to encourage your child to use *context, memory*, and *letter-sounds* or *word parts*. Ask, "What word would make sense in that sentence (context meaning)? Do you remember seeing that word or one that looks like it (memory)? Can you think of a meaningful word which has that letter-sound at the beginning (letter-sounds)?"

**Word-Meaning**: In addition to observing a student's approach to recognizing words, we need to watch how well a child understands the meanings of words and phrases. For example, observe as your child reads a list of words or a few short sentences. You can see and hear more than how a child may be recognizing the words. Your child may be showing you a need for understanding the *meanings* of words. When reading words in a list, does your child just say a "nonsense" word, a word which has no meaning?

I remember a third grader, Andy, who read ten words in a list to me and then a brief story. He read five of the ten words correctly. On the five he missed, he said, "chiz" for *chess*, "dirt-ton" for *direction*, "slamp" for *slump*, "chif" for *chief*, and "dar" for *dear*. He read at a steady rate, rarely hesitating at a word. It never seemed to bother him that he was not saying meaningful words. He would do the same in a story—just say what he thought the word looked like. He rarely appeared to listen to hear whether or not the word was meaningful. When I read some of the words correctly to Andy, he knew the meanings of a few. Yet, I shared with him how important it is to listen to himself and try to use meaningful words. Otherwise, he would just be saying "nonsense" words. His understanding of stories was suffering because he did not attempt to read meaningful words.

Through my experiences, I have seen students sending *signals* telling us they have strengths and needs in word recognition, vocabulary, and other reading and language areas. We can spot some of those signals and begin to see more of how reading and language are interrelated by using the guidelines offered in Section Two. We should not become overwhelmed by details. We need to always encourage students to aim at the major goals related to PURE Reading success: Purpose, Understanding, good Recall, and Enjoyment.

## SUMMARY: GAINING INFORMATION

In this first phase of The Language Triangle, I have shared how children gain information through *listening* and *reading*. Chapter One emphasized that children need to listen to someone explain the meaning of sights and sounds. Remember five-month-old Joe whose mother Mary eagerly began telling her son more about what he was seeing and hearing? Then there was Jerry, the eleven-year-old. He appeared to need help in reading, but his broader need was in the area of language understanding. Jerry needed to listen carefully and understand what he heard, so the words and ideas would be more meaningful as he read.

Chapter Two provided the four keys to reading success: (1) Purpose, (2) Understanding, (3) good Recall, and (4) Enjoyment — PURE Reading. These factors can be cultivated from early first encounters with reading through every stage of reading development.

Gaining information, however, is merely the beginning. Unless we understand and communicate that information, The Language Triangle is incomplete. Let's move on to Part Two to see how the *Understanding* portion of the triangle is formed.

# Part Two

## UNDERSTANDING

THE SECOND PHASE of The Language Triangle involves (2) UNDERSTANDING the meaning of the world around us.

Children are daily bombarded by exciting new sights and sounds. In their eagerness to learn, children ask, "What, Why, How . . .?" Their enthusiasm and memory for new experiences will fade quickly, however, unless they understand what they see and hear. Understanding or *meaning* usually comes by (1) Thinking On Our Own; (2) having Time to Think; and (3) Getting Involved when learning.

# 3

# THINKING ON OUR OWN

*The Language Triangle*

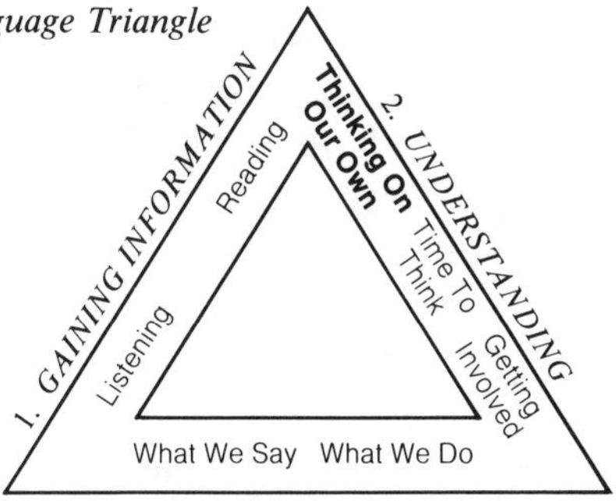


WE ALL ENCOUNTER new experiences daily. In order to understand the new experience best, we either (1) depend on someone to share its meaning, or (2) we figure out the meaning on our own.

## DEPENDING ON SOMEONE

Earlier I shared an experience about my friend who was eager to get her son, Joe, ready to read. We talked about how important it was to talk and actually get Joe involved in the new experience. Active listening opportunities are essential if children are to understand each new encounter. We all *depend* on someone to share meaning at first. Try not to let others discourage you from providing information to very young children and infants, as I saw happen recently.

I attended a baby shower for a mother and her infant daughter, Jennie, who was not quite two months old. Jennie was a very alert little one, looking about at all the faces and turning quickly when she heard a new sound. As her mother opened the gifts, Carol, a friend, was holding Jennie. The gifts were passed around and as they came to where Jennie was, Carol would tell Jennie in a very excited way what new present she now possessed. After three or four gifts passed, a few of those sitting nearby began to tease Carol. "Jennie is too young to understand" was the general consensus.

It didn't take long before Carol stopped telling Jennie about the gifts. How sad! I was sitting across the crowded room, and I didn't want to break the excitment by declaring, "Jennie needs someone to tell her about her gifts, so she will recognize them when she hears her mother talk about them and show them to her later." I did give Carol an encouraging word later.

We all need someone to guide and help us understand those things with which we have had no experience. The explanation can never begin too early. Parents who begin when their children appear "too young to understand" will be amazed when, at a later time, without warning, the child will demonstrate understanding. This seemingly incredible memory among young children may be more common than we have believed possible. We won't realize the possibilities until we begin to share more with them at a younger age — and then listen and watch.

Ruth, a friend of mine, shared a recent experience in which her two-year-old daughter, Sarah, left Ruth shaking her head in disbelief. Ruth and I were having lunch sometime last January when she told me of taking Sarah to Frankenmuth, Michigan, the previous August. (Frankenmuth is a community in eastern Michigan featuring, among other things, a store with large Christmas displays.) They saw Christmas displays which are available year-round. Sarah, who was not quite two at the time, was speaking in two and three-word sentences ("Go by-by," "Me want bottle," . . .). Her words were two or three syllables long at the most. Sarah was delighted and overwhelmed by the Frankenmuth experience. She showed her joy through her actions. She would squeal in excitment, but she said little else. Ruth remembers telling Sarah that they were in Frankenmuth, and "These are the kinds of things you will see at Christmas time." In Sarah's presence, Ruth told everyone how much her daughter had enjoyed the visit to Frankenmuth. Ruth can't recall saying much about it after the middle of September. Then in mid-December, the family was decorating the Christmas tree. Without prompting or any warning, Sarah stood before the brightly-lit tree and yelled in a voice of utter delight, "JUST LIKE FAK-MOOF!" Can you imagine the shock?

I am not suggesting that all youngsters have that good a memory, but we need to allow for the possibilities. We won't know how much children will understand and remember until we give them the opportunity. Tell them about the world around them. Listen and watch what happens!

As your child grows, there will always be situations which will call upon you to explain new experiences, unfamiliar words, unusual circumstances, strange sounds . . . Even though we never outgrow the need to depend on someone, we should eventually do more thinking on our own.

## FIGURING OUT MEANING ON OUR OWN

Even though your child will always depend on someone for certain explanations and guidance, how can you help your child think more independently? How can children be guided into doing things without depending on someone for a step-by-step explanation?

**Forgetfulness**: Many so-called "forgetful" people are really individuals who may have depended too much and too long on being told what to do. When there are chores to be done, assignments to be completed . . . does your child constantly SEEM to forget what to do? We have all heard of a "Janet" who "forgets" it's her turn to do dishes on Tuesday, and "Dan" who "forgets" to take his turn on Wednesdays.

There *are* cases when such memory lapses can be considered problems and may be signs of deeper learning difficulties; BUT, I have found that many of those who appear to have poor memories have one or a combination of two things happening in their daily lives:

1. The individual fails to do tasks completely unless told exactly what should be done.

2. The individual has someone who is willing to tell what should be done.

Few individuals realize that they are so dependent, and even fewer recognize their role in keeping someone dependent on them. Or at least very few will admit it.

**Ask More — Tell Less**: So what do we do about those who depend too much and too long? TRY TO ASK MORE and TELL LESS. It takes more time and patience to ask, "Janet, do you know what today is? What responsibility do you have on Tuesdays?"

This may seem too simple, but notice something. When we always tell our child to do something, we have done most of the thinking about what, when, and how something should be done. By asking questions and waiting for an answer, our child has to do more thinking. This applies to young and old:

*Asking The Young Child*: It would be ideal if we could all start by using the "ask more" approach with our children in infancy or when they were very young.

I was at a park recently with the mothers of two toddlers, Lynn and Doug, both two and a half years old. Lynn's mother guided her from slide to merry-go-round telling her, "Be careful, take one step at a time." "Don't let go of the slide on the way down." "Let's go to the merry-go-round." "Sit in the middle of the merry-go-round, so you don't fall off."

Doug's mother was also close by as Doug was about to climb the steps of the slide. She asked, "Now how are you supposed to go up the steps and slide down so you won't hurt yourself?" He didn't say a word, but he carefully took one step at a time as his mother praised him for being careful. After a few turns at the slide, she asked, "Well, where should we go next?"

He ran to the merry-go-round with his mother close behind. Doug's mother then asked, "Now where should you sit so you can hold on tight and not slide around?"

Doug jumped on to the merry-go-round, up and over the restraining bars. He plopped himself into the center against the inside bars as he said, "Here!" His mother responded with, "You're so right!" She gave him a big smile as she began to spin him.

Doug's mother had developed a style of questioning and not telling. This gave Doug an opportunity to think and do what he should without always being told. His words and actions showed his mother how well he could think and understand on his own. His mother's reactions let him know he was doing the right thing.

***The Older Child And Adult***: If you live with a teenager or adult who has depended heavily on being told what to do, you know that it's hard to break old habits. It will be frustrating and rather aggravating at times if you begin questioning and not telling all at once.

Start slowly — experiment. Definitely praise your child when the task is complete. Let him know you recognized and appreciated the slightest part of what was done independently. Things will not change overnight. We need to recognize that thinking takes time.

# 4

# TIME TO THINK

*The Language Triangle*

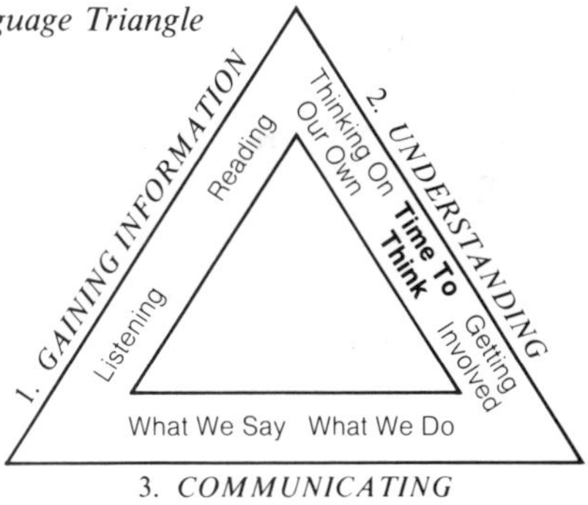


WHETHER WE ARE depending on someone or trying to figure out meaning on our own, we all need *time to think*. I realize that in an emergency situation, we don't have as much thinking time as we would like, but we are taught, even in those situations, to think before we act.

If we are relying on someone to explain meaning, our helper needs to *allow time* for us to think, or if we are able to figure out the meaning on our own, we need to *take time* to think.

**ALLOW TIME**

I remember recently having a little girl, Beth, who was about one year old visit me with her mother. I was boiling a pot of water on the stove. Beth's mother told me she had not succeeded in teaching Beth the meaning of "hot," so we needed to watch Beth closely.

I thought I would be bold and try to teach Beth the concept of "hot." I pointed to the steamy pot on the stove, placed my hand near it, and put on a regular theatrical performance trying to demonstrate what "hot" meant. When finished, I was proud of how attentive Beth had been during my *act*. So I asked, "Beth, what do you do when something is HOT?" My ego wanted her to immediately jump away from the stove with her hands thrown in the air, exclaiming "HOT" as she jumped.

No such thing happened. She looked at me, then walked

nonchalantly to her mother. I went on with my cooking while Beth's mother and I talked.

A few minutes later, Beth walked over to me with her fingers in her mouth. She took them out to pull shyly on my skirt. As I looked down at her, she glanced quickly at her mother, at me, and then at the pan of boiling water. She hesitantly raised her hand and seemed to jerk it away as I had done. I hugged her and said, "YES, that's what you do when it's HOT!" She smiled and ran to her mother for a very special hug. After that she slowly began associating the word HOT with other things as her mother and father showed her a HOT fireplace, HOT toaster, HOT coffee pot . . .

Beth had needed time to look over the situation and think. She needed time to remember and associate other situations like the one with my pot. She may have recalled her mother showing her the steam from HOT cereal, the kettle of HOT water on their stove . . . Her mother had probably acted in a way similar to the theatrics she had just witnessed. Children will learn and associate ideas in different ways and at different rates, but we shouldn't give up . . . as I had that day with Beth.

## TAKE TIME

Some of us need to take more time to think. Many of us tend to react before taking that necessary time.

I remember this would be the greatest frustration for a thirteen-year-old girl named Christine. As soon as Chris would hear a question begin, she would jump in with an answer before the teacher had time to finish. When she attempted reading new words, she would blurt out the first thing that came to her mind.

I worked hard trying to help Christine *pace herself* and take sufficient time to be more accurate. She needed to learn to use *thinking time*. To help Chris, I talked with her parents and teacher. We all would tell Chris, whenever it seemed appropriate, that she was not allowed to answer a question until she was given a cue to respond. She was challenged to hold back the answer until we either nodded our heads, patted her softly on the shoulder, smiled at her, or whispered a soft, "ok." All these were cues, which were never threatening. They were reassuring ways to let her know that it was all right to answer, since she had taken time to think. Other ideas which I have seen help students take more time to think are offered in Section Two under *Organization*.

# 5

# GETTING INVOLVED

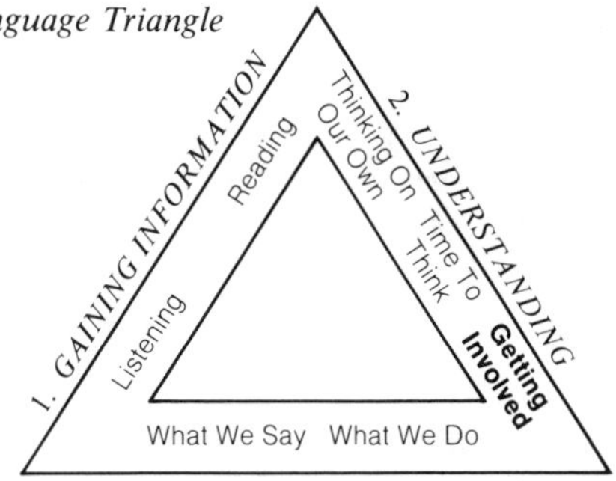

*The Language Triangle*

AS OUR CHILDREN begin to understand more by thinking on their own and taking time to think, we are still left with the desire to have them understand, remember, and enjoy more of what they experience. But HOW?

## ACTIVELY PARTICIPATE

I recently saw a television news report about "children television addicts." The mother of one seven year old said her son would sit before the T.V. set without moving or talking for two and three hours at a time! The reporter interviewed a counselor who suggested that one of the most effective techniques for decreasing viewing time was to encourage children to actively play and participate in interesting, meaningful activities. To emphasize this point, one boy was shown smiling as he played with an electric train. I felt like shouting, "Now a T.V. report is telling us that children need to be active — not passive — listeners and watchers. Why can't our parental logic tell us the same thing?"

I know how tempting it is to allow the television to occupy our children so we can get things done or get some rest. But it frightens me to think what we could be doing. By satisfying our needs, our children sit quietly inactive. If we want our children to understand, remember, and enjoy what they are to learn, they need opportunities to do more than see and hear. We need to encourage and guide our children as they *touch, smell, taste, talk about, even write about* . . . new experiences. They need to be active participants in learning.

**GUIDED INVOLVEMENT**

Did I say, "TOUCH?" Yes, I know that we are accustomed to having a "hands-off" policy about breakable and valuable items. Yet, children are curious. Such curiosity often gets them in trouble unless we guide them.

A friend, Sue, had her 18-month-old granddaughter, Pam, visiting her for the day when I stopped for a few minutes. She had some valuable antique dolls well within Pam's reach. I was amazed at how Pam would go up to a doll occasionally, pat it softly, then run off to play. She never tried to pick one up. I was amazed! I asked Sue why Pam wasn't bothering these valuable antiques. She explained that before Pam was 6 months old, she noticed the baby looking at the dolls. Sue would pick up the doll and bring it to Pam. Sue would gently hold Pam's hand and let her stroke the face, the dress, and the hair of the doll as Sue told the baby about what she was touching. She told Pam that these were special dolls to see and touch softly. They weren't for play. Then Sue would give Pam a toy that could be tossed, squeezed, hugged . . . As the baby grew and could crawl and then walk to the dolls, she needed reminders about treating them gently. Sue would always try to offer another toy in its place.

Gradually, Sue noticed that Pam would go to the dolls, softly touch one and then go to play. She would give Pam a big hug and praise her in some way when she was careful with the dolls.

I know that things don't always go smoothly after giving our children explanations or opportunities to touch under our supervision. Yet, I have noticed that such explanations and guided experience do help if we are patient and don't give up.

Children of all ages are curious. By guiding them to touch or handle something carefully while letting them know how special the object is, it seems to satisfy some of the curiosity. We are also providing them with important experiences that help them understand more about the world around them.

## SUMMARY: UNDERSTANDING

In this second phase of The Language Triangle, I have stressed that our children's enjoyment and memory for new experiences will fade unless they have an adequate understanding of that experience.

Understanding comes by *Thinking On Our Own* — but at first we will depend on others to guide and explain new experiences. Such explanations can never come too early, and there will be occasions throughout our lives when we will depend on someone to explain a new experience. Eventually, we should think more on our own. Some people who appear "forgetful" are really depending too long and too much on being told what to do. To help them think more on their own, we need to ASK MORE and TELL LESS.

Whether we are depending on someone, or thinking on our own, we all need *Time to Think*. If we are explaining the meaning to someone, we need to ALLOW TIME for that person to understand. If we are figuring the meaning on our own, we need to TAKE TIME to think.

I also shared that our children need to do more than listen and watch if they are to remember, understand, and enjoy what they learn. They need to *Get Involved* in what they are learning. Encourage and guide your child to become actively involved in ways that will make an experience more meaningful.

Once we have had the opportunity to UNDERSTAND more about the world around us, we need to COMMUNICATE that understanding. Such communication completes The Language Triangle — the next part will explain how this can be accomplished.

# Part Three

## COMMUNICATING

THE THIRD PHASE of The Language Triangle involves (3) COMMUNICATING by what we say and do.

If your child appears to be a good listener, an excellent reader, and a deep thinker — that's not enough! A child may be taking in good information, but each person needs to communicate by what is said or done. I recognize that communication is a means of expressing our needs, but it is more than that. It is a way of knowing what learning has occurred — and what new ideas an individual can create.

# 6

# WHAT WE SAY

*The Language Triangle*

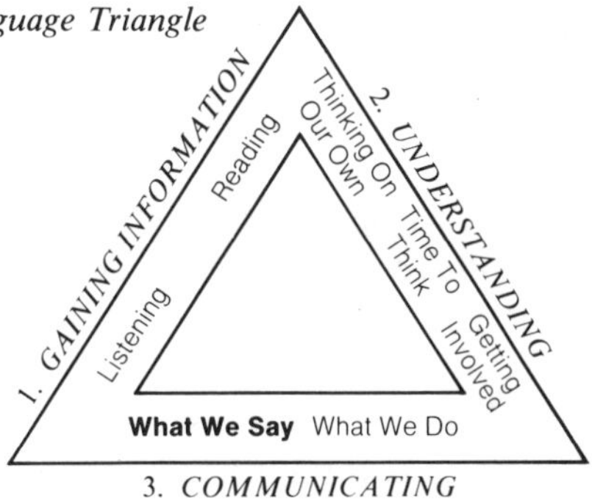


YOU MAY BE uncertain whether or not your child understands the meaning of a new experience unless you encourage your child to tell you what has been learned.

## AN INFANT OR YOUNG CHILD

Children under the age of two or three communicate by what they *say*. Even though full words cannot always be spoken clearly, young children can *speak*. David Pushaw[1] gives parents specific information about a child's speech development. Let me offer some general ideas to keep in mind as we think of the young child learning to speak.

**Before A Year**: Even before a baby forms syllables, a first means of communicating or telling us what is needed comes through crying. Most of us could tell whether our child's cry meant hunger, pain, a desire for attention . . . It was a first attempt at communicating through the use of sounds.

Did you notice that crying gradually gave way to other sounds? I can remember how I enjoyed hearing our daughter, Anne, when she was two to three months old begin *talking*. Her voice would get soft and loud forming sounds which seemed to imitate our speech, but of course, she wasn't saying anything in the form of syllables or words. She looked intently at us and seemed engrossed in a very important conversation as she *spoke*. When she paused, my husband or I would fill in with a question or comment about what we were doing. We acted as though we understood everything she was saying, nodding our heads in agreement and smiling as we spoke with her. Our conversations would become very long, especially after she woke from a nap or a long night's sleep. Eventually, she began to make the sounds of "ba-ba, . . . da-da, . . . ma-ma." Have you noticed that most babies will repeat those sounds which cause a "ma-ma" and "da-da" to jump for joy and get excited? If we say the words back to our children, they will be more apt to repeat the sounds.

I have heard of situations in which children have said those sounds, but the parents tell me the child stopped. The child never seemed to say them again until much later, if at all. In many cases, a delay between the first and next time a sound is made is quite normal. In other cases, where the sounds were never pronounced again, it may have been because the baby had a hearing problem, or may not have had someone get excited and repeat the words to give the positive assurance which is essential.

**Sounds Become Words**: We soon hear a child form sounds and words which are meaningful to the child but not always understood by others. For example, our Anne would say, "la, la" for *flower*, "lo, lo" for *Cheerios*.

I discovered how easy it would be and sometimes how cute it would sound if I spoke using her words. I had to remind myself, however, that I was not doing Anne any favors by letting her hear the incorrect pronunciation of "flower" or "Cheerios."

She understood me whether I used her word or the correct pronunciation. I realized that if I wanted her to eventually say the words correctly, she would need to hear them pronounced properly.

As she grew and began to remember more words with their sequence of complex sounds, she could say the words distinctly and more clearly.

If we continue to use the child's words when speaking, we are preventing our child from hearing the words which should eventually be pronounced correctly. *Don't get caught in that trap*. Hearing and using correct language provides a strong basis for future reading success.

**Sounds And Inflections**: There are other sounds besides those necessary to form words which are important for children to hear and imitate. Animal sounds, sounds of airplanes, cars passing, steam hissing — all provide a child with opportunities to practice sounds which will help in forming words.

We also need to give children opportunities to use different tones as they speak. They need to hear us emphasize sounds in different ways. Speak in a whisper. Get excited and cheer loudly for a winning team. Encourage your child to do the same. Use definite *highs* and *lows* or inflections in your speech. The child can learn to hear where certain syllables within words and words in sentences should be stressed. Remember, we are the examples. Laugh, giggle, be stern, be happy . . . A child can be that way, too.

## THE OLDER CHILD

After children are two to three years of age, marked differences are seen in their understanding and use of language. What had been individual syllables or sounds will become phrases and sentences. Even though they once imitated most of the sounds which they said, children will begin more and more conversation on their own. Parents will begin to say, "Where did you learn that?" As children grow, we need to remember that they need to be encouraged to speak. If such opportunities for speaking and conversing are not provided, there could be a noticeable breakdown in a student's reading and language growth.

I can remember a high school student who attended a reading clinic which I directed one summer. He was three to four years below his grade level in overall reading development. After looking into his background we found that in this student's home children were not allowed to speak, unless they were spoken to. Silence was considered *golden*. It was not a punishment. It was a standard of behavior which was respected by family members.

As a result of this home environment, the children were not given enough opportunities to use and experience language. We knew that the student with whom we were working was using short sentences, incorrect grammar, improper names or labels for objects, and other signs of a language need.

His father was obviously a strong believer in the philosophy of silence. We explained that unless his son had opportunities to speak and apply those ideas which he heard and read, he would continue to fall behind in his reading achievement. Since the father's standards also included a desire to have his son become a successful reader, he faced a dilemma. Should he break a well-established standard which he supported by allowing this son to speak more in the home? Or should he maintain the standard of silence and sacrifice reading achievement?

He decided to see if his son could improve without the necessary practice in speaking. He said he made this decision because his younger sons did not seem to be suffering, and he needed to maintain the respect of the family. We agreed that it might be possible for some students to succeed without the needed practice in speaking because of such a wide range of differences in the ways in which we learn.

Later that summer we met one of the younger sons and informally observed that he was showing many of the same signs as his older brother. The gap in his reading achievement was not as great because he was younger. He showed every sign of falling farther and farther behind. We shared this with the father, but he didn't change his mind.

I am glad that most situations I have encountered have not ended with the degree of frustration which I feel when I think of the children in that home. In fact, I find myself meeting more and more parents who say that they have a youngster who talks all the time but is not reading well. In those cases, the child needs to be observed closely. A child's needs in terms of language and reading can be observed using the guidelines such as those offered in Section Two of this book.

Communicating through *what we say* is one way of demonstrating our understanding of what we gained from participating in listening and reading experiences. We communicate in other ways also, as we will see in the next chapter.

Reference:

[1] Pushaw, David. *Teach Your Child to Talk: A Parent's Guide*. Cebco Standard Publishers. New York, 1976 (Paperback).

# 7

# WHAT WE DO

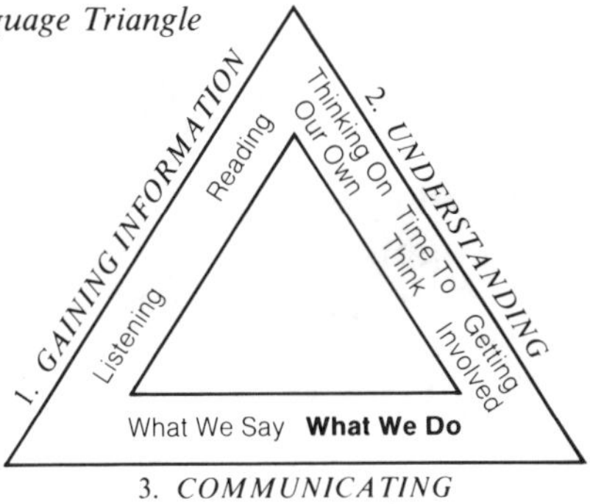


*The Language Triangle*

OUR CHILDREN communicate an understanding of the world around us by what they do as well as what they say. Their actions send signals which tell those around them how well they understand and feel about what is happening.

In this chapter, I will share the *signals children send* when they don't say a word. I will also discuss how children communicate by *drawing and writing*.

## SIGNALS CHILDREN SEND

Children are resourceful in finding ways of communicating through their actions. We need to be alert to their signals.

Many infants show an interest in things around them by trying to turn toward certain sights and sounds. Exact gestures such as pointing may not come until well after a child is a year old in some cases, while other children become very exact in their "signals" before that. Bright, moving, noisy objects are especially interesting to infants. Watch how your child shows an interest in things. A baby's head may turn or whole body may twist. Some children kick enthusiastically or wave their arms as though reaching for something, even though they may not be extending their arms in the exact direction of the object. Remember, your child will depend on you at first to explain what is seen and heard. It is best if you begin by explaining those things in which your child has shown an interest.

Your baby may show an interest in the light in the nursery.

After you talk about the light, you can find out whether or not your baby understands by asking, "Where is the LIGHT?" Watch and see what happens. At a very young age, before your child is a year old, a baby's eyes and body may turn toward the light, or show understanding by sending signals such as those I mentioned earlier. BE ALERT! A baby won't always do as you expect — but your child may be letting you know, "I understand!"

If you see that your baby recognizes the light, praise. . . hug . . . let your little one know you agree, "YES, that's the LIGHT." If your child hasn't reacted, after allowing time to think, point to the light and say, "This is the LIGHT."

There are many times when we least expect children to show us they understand. I remember an experience with my friend Diane's baby, Mike. Diane was changing Mike on the table in his room as we were talking about the picture of the bear hanging above his crib. Mike was about five or six months old at the time. We noticed that he was trying to twist and turn so he could face his crib. Diane was having a terrible time getting him to stay still for the diaper change, until we realized where he was really looking.

His eyes kept seeking out the bear on the wall above his crib. When his mother turned him so he could see the bear clearly, he stopped twisting, and the diaper change was completed without any fuss. He had heard us mention the bear. Since his parents had acquainted him with the various things in his room, he was showing us he understood! Neither Diane nor I were prepared for him to show such understanding, especially since we had not singled-out the word "bear." It had been included in the flurry of words as a part of our conversation. This experience immediately reminded me that I should never underestimate a young child's ability to understand and communicate.

## DRAWING AND WRITING

Children should always be given opportunities to express themselves through actions. As your child grows, however, there is no better way to provide a strong basis for success in reading and all language experiences than through drawing and writing.

By drawing and writing, your child is putting to work important ingredients of The Language Triangle — listening, reading, understanding, speaking. *Drawing* provides the opportunity for your child to communicate about something that has been seen and no doubt heard. As your child tells you about the picture, the ability to communicate by what is said is being strengthened. When writing, your child has the opportunity to use words and ideas which have been heard, spoken, understood, and read. By sharing what has been learned by listening and reading, your child is restating what others may have said and written. Children need to be encouraged to do more than that.

**The Ultimate Goal - Creativity:** The ultimate goal should be to encourage your child to communicate creative ideas independently. As your child shares ideas by drawing and writing, others will have the opportunity to listen, read, understand, and think about what your child has communicated. Thus, your child's creative efforts provide the means for helping others exercise important ingredients of The Language Triangle.

Experience tells us that drawing and writing come easier for some than for others. Regardless of how easy or hard it appears to be for your child to draw or write, be assured that individuals can best reach the goal of creativity if we offer guidance at first, and then whenever it is needed.

**Drawing - They Need The Experience**: Just as placing books with paper pages into the hands of a young child can stir the anxiety of any parent, so can putting crayons or pencils into their hands cause fears — unless the child is being watched by someone who can ensure their proper use.

If children see someone writing or drawing, they usually want to do the same. We need to look at the advantages of giving them experiences, rather than dwell on the disastrous results which occur if the child is not watched closely.

Children usually have many chances to strengthen their

larger muscles which are used for crawling, walking, throwing, running . . ., but fewer experiences are offered in which they can exercise and strengthen the small or "fine" muscles used for drawing and writing.

I have heard some children complain or cry in pain when they have not done much coloring or drawing before they get to school. Most adults think it is a child's way of getting out of hard work. But if we, as adults, don't use our large muscles required for jogging or racquet ball, we are in terrible pain the day after our first workout. We expect the sympathy and understanding of all those around us. Don't children deserve the same consideration!

Some youngsters avoid writing and drawing activities. They may not be interested because they have not been introduced to the fun of coloring, drawing, writing . . . Or a child may reason that since he has succeeded so far in running, jumping, throwing and other large muscle activities, why do something which will only bring frustration?

It is hard for someone to force a child to do something which is difficult, so the best solution is to (1) OFFER A LITTLE EXPERIENCE AT A TIME, and (2) MAKE THE EXPERIENCE AS POSITIVE AS POSSIBLE.

Don't expect a child who avoids drawing and writing to do as much in the same amount of time as youngsters who succeeded in these types of activities in the past. Guide the child by helping draw or write things which are easy at first and become gradually harder as one begins to taste success.

Children as young as two or three should be given crayons and blank sheets of paper on which they can scribble and draw. Start with a blank paper so the child can be creative. The person who is watching should be actively involved giving encouragement and praise whenever possible. As children grow, they usually go through various stages as they "draw."

At first, youngsters will use crayons, paints, and other drawing tools (1) *just for fun and to get your reaction*. Eventually, at about two or three years of age, they will (2) *name what has been drawn after it is finished*. As children get older, they will (3) *name what they are doing while they are drawing*. Finally, you will notice your child (4) *naming what will be drawn before it is begun*. Watch and listen. Praise your child for whatever is being done — whether it's just for the fun of it or for a planned purpose!

**Some Need A Model**: On occasion, show children how pictures are formed. Rather than first giving a child a coloring book in which all the pictures and words are already on the page, your child should occasionally watch as someone draws a picture or writes a word. We often assume that children know how pictures and words got onto the page, but some of them will need time before they make the connection between what they see as a completed picture and what they are capable of drawing themselves. Occasionally show them.

As you draw you should tell your child what you are drawing. If you are drawing a face, say, ''I am going to draw a face. Here is the head, here are the eyes, the eyebrows, the mouth . . .'' Before the age of two or three, ask your little one to point to the eyes, the eyebrows, the mouth . . . when you finish. As children get older, give them crayons. Some children will draw on their own. Others can be guided by asking, ''Where can you put the mouth, ears . . .?''

This should only be done occasionally. Children should not always rely on someone to show them how to draw or write, but it may be done now and then in the beginning.

**Forming Letters and Words**: When children are in school, we often assume that if students see the letter-charts in the front of a classroom or on the wall of a bedroom, they will know how to make the letters when they print or write. It is clear that some children may need a model to show them how to draw even the most simple objects at times, so we can't assume that they will automatically know how to form complex letters.

Just as a child's drawings progress in stages, writing grows with time and experience. Before two or three years of age, your child can learn by watching as you write. In early attempts to write, a child creates lines which flow in various patterns on a page — circles, bumps, repeated "scratches" . . . If given lined paper, the beginner ignores the boundaries the lines form. As youngsters gain more experience by watching and imitating, they will eventually make their writing flow between the lines. This comes as a child grows and watches others write. It should not be forced in a way that pressures a child into moving from one stage to another.

At about five or six years of age (and before that for those who appear ready), children can begin to be guided comfortably through four stages of what I call, "Learning to Form Letters and Words." A child needs to be guided in one or a combination of the four stages.

## LEARNING TO FORM LETTERS AND WORDS

| | |
|---|---|
| **STAGE ONE: TRACE-OVER** | Copy directly over what has been written. |
| **STAGE TWO: CLOSE-RANGE** | (1) Same paper: Copying below or next to what has been written on the same paper.<br>(2) Different paper: Copying from one paper to another on the same table or desk. |
| **STAGE THREE: DISTANT-COPYING** | Copying from the chalkboard, charts, or anywhere which requires the following:<br>(1) Looking away from the writing paper.<br>(2) Seeing letters or words at a distance beyond the desk or table.<br>(3) Remembering what is to be copied as the student looks back to the writing paper.<br>(4) Forming letters and words correctly. |
| **STAGE FOUR: ON YOUR OWN** | Letters and words can be written without needing to look at a model. |

Stage Three is more complex than the first two stages. Individuals who have trouble seeing at a distance, remembering what they see, and/or cannot form words correctly are easily frustrated with "distant-copying." If a student is having trouble at Stage Three, we should consider doing the following: (1) check vision; (2) encourage the child to say what is to be remembered (thus, the child will hear and see what is to be copied); (3) offer assignments at Stages One and Two. Our goal must be to have children become independent in knowing how to write, but this independence will not come at the same rate for all children.

I have found that forming letters is one of the areas in which improvement can be seen quickly if a child is *willing and ready* to improve. Three things are necessary to stimulate improvement in the individual who is forming letters incorrectly and is willing and ready to progress: (1) The students need to know what letters are being formed incorrectly. (2) Someone needs to show how the letters are to be formed. (3) The student needs practice writing correctly at times other than the writing lesson — and a child needs to be praised when something has been written correctly without a reminder. When your child encounters problems with the mechanics of writing, you may find the observations and suggested activities offered under "*Writing and Drawing*" in Section Two helpful.

**Creating With Guidance**: As I mentioned earlier in this chapter, every child should be encouraged to create stories using his own ideas. I do not want to leave you with the impression that drawing and writing should always be an act which is imitated and mechanical. Creativity should be the ultimate goal, but some need guidance as they try to reach that goal.

The Language Experience Approach offers opportunities for individuals of all ages to receive some guidance as they create stories based on experience. I introduced the approach in Chapter Two, where I briefly described how to use it with young children. I have used the Language Experience Approach, however, with individuals of all ages — preschool through adulthood. For further details beyond those offered in Chapter Two, please see what Russell Stauffer[2] and Roach Van Allen[3] suggest when using this approach with children. Anabel Newman[4] gives excellent guidance in using Language Experience stories with adults who need help in reading.

This approach offers the unique opportunity for an individual to apply the three major areas of The Language Triangle. An individual (1) gains information through an experience and (2) shows an understanding of the experience by (3) communicating through what one says and possibly draws. As an individual describes the experience, someone writes the story. Eventually, the individual may write the story independently. Thus, each person can go through the "triangle" again by (1) reading (gaining information) from what was written, (2) thinking and understanding what was read as it was (3) shared with others (communicating).

We don't want our children to always rely on someone to do the writing for them, but the Language Experience Approach can help encourage the creativity by guiding them at first. The human mind has a wealth of creativity which needs to be encouraged.

## SUMMARY: COMMUNICATING

Communication is often considered a means of expressing needs, BUT it is more than that. In this third phase of The Language Triangle I stressed that communication, through what we say and do, tells others what we have learned — and provides the opportunity to express creative ideas.

Your child will communicate by what is said from infancy. You need to set a good example as your child learns to pronounce words correctly. You must also provide opportunities for your child to speak. If your child fails to meaningfully use the words eventually seen in print, reading will become an act of saying words which have not been experienced, and therefore, the words have no meaning.

Also from infancy, our children will be communicating by what they do. Watch for the signals they send to show what interests them. Then we need to be alert as our children show us they understand something we have taken the time to explain to them. Your child will eventually communicate more through drawing and writing. Our ultimate goal should be to have children communicate their own, creative ideas through drawing and writing, but children may need guidance at first. We need to WATCH AND POSITIVELY RESPOND TO WHAT THEY ARE READY AND ABLE TO DO. Even though your child may need that guidance in the beginning, always encourage the creation of pictures and stories using your child's own ideas.

[2] Stauffer, Russell. *The Language Experience Approach to the Teaching of Reading*. Harper and Row. New York, 1970.

[3] Allen, Roach Van and Claryce Allen. *An Introduction to a Language Experience Program*. Encyclopedia Britannica Press, 1966.

[4] Newman, Anabel. *Adult Basic Education*. Allyn Bacon, Inc. Boston, 1980.

*The Language Triangle*

# SECTION ONE: THE LANGUAGE TRIANGLE

## Summary

When I asked parents to read and react to what I have shared in Section One, each person recalled ideas or situations which applied best to their children. That's as it should be.

Think back over what you have read and reflect on those areas which made you say to yourself, "I needed that."

**Introduction**: When we say, "I want my child to read better," we must recognize that reading is part of a broader picture which I have called The Language Triangle. If we try to teach reading without recognizing how reading is related to the broader area of language, we will be spinning our wheels and getting nowhere.

**Gaining Information**: Children gain new language information through listening and reading. If they attempt reading words which they have never heard and understood, they will be saying sounds which are meaningless. We can never put too much stress on guiding our children as they gain experience in hearing and understanding language. We will experience the pay-off when a child reads a new word and looks up to say, "Oh, I know what that means, I've heard it before."

We also gain information through reading. Keep in mind the four keys to reading success. We need to have a (1) Purpose for reading and we need to (2) Understand, (3) Recall, and (4) Enjoy what we read — **PURE** Reading.

**Understanding**: If children are to understand, remember, and enjoy new experiences, they need to (1) Think on Their Own, (2) have Time to Think, and (3) Get Involved in what they are to learn.

**Communicating**: As parents we need to encourage our children to share what they have learned and express their creative ideas by what they say and what they do. We can never assume that learning has occurred or creativity is present because a student appears to listen and read carefully. Each child demonstrates what he has learned and shares his creativity by what he shows us or tells us!

Most parents with whom I have had the pleasure of discussing The Language Triangle grasp the ideas and see how reading is related to this broader language picture. To a person, however, their primary interest is in how they can best apply this information in their own situation.

The next section of this book is designed to put The Reading Triangle (parent, child, and teacher) to work in applying what I have shared in Section One.

# SECTION TWO

## PUTTING THE READING TRIANGLE TO WORK

# PUTTING THE READING TRIANGLE TO WORK

## Introduction

I AM SURE that you picked up this book because you want to help your child succeed in reading. I believe that our good intentions and good ideas are effective, however, only when we are (1) informed, and (2) involved. Section One, The Language Triangle, informed you as to how reading cannot be isolated from the rest of your child's language experiences. Section Two offers a practical way to involve you, your child, and the teacher — The Reading Triangle — in working together to make reading a successful and enjoyable adventure. The suggestions in this section are designed for school-age children — kindergarten and older.

Section Two is divided into three parts:

Part One: *Guidelines for Communication* suggests that members of The Reading Triangle need to communicate if a child is to improve in reading. Ten guidelines are offered to help achieve this goal.

Part Two: *The Reading Log* offers a sample of how you can keep an informal record of your child's progress.

Part Three: *Observations and Activities* provides a wealth of practical information in eight reading and language areas.

Those who have read this section before this book was published commented on how full of ideas it is, BUT I was strongly encouraged to suggest that you read through the entire section to get an overview of what it has to offer. I was told how tempting it was to skip through to find those portions which caught the interest of the reader, but my readers have found it more beneficial to review all of Section Two and see how everything is related. After you have read through the entire section, go back. Consider more carefully all the guidelines in Part One and The Reading Log suggested in Part Two. Then choose those portions of Part Three which best meet your child's situation, and apply what is offered by putting to work the guidelines offered in Part One.

# Part One

## GUIDELINES FOR COMMUNICATION

THE FOLLOWING guidelines are presented as a means of helping you, your child, and the teacher communicate. So many times when you find books, articles, or speakers with activities or programs for improving reading, you may diligently try some of the ideas, but you are never sure whether you are doing the right thing. When your child doesn't seem to make progress, you are left frustrated. I don't want to leave you that way. I believe that *communication* between home and school is essential. Without it, you may be stressing one thing to help with reading, and the school may be emphasizing another. Your child is caught in the middle of the confusion.

The following ten guidelines are offered as a means of providing you with insight and information. They are designed to improve communication between home and school, so your child's reading and language will grow. PLEASE READ THE FOLLOWING GUIDELINES CAREFULLY BEFORE YOU TRY ANY OF THE ACTIVITIES YOU WILL SEE LATER IN THIS SECTION:

1. **Recognize the keys to reading success.** A successful reader has a PURPOSE for reading and a desire to UNDERSTAND, RECALL, and ENJOY what is read — **PURE** Reading.

2. **Look more closely at your child's daily behavior** as it relates to the various areas of language and reading as shared in Section One of this book. How well does your child LISTEN, READ, UNDERSTAND, and COMMUNICATE? No special testing should be necessary at first to recognize what your child is doing in each language area.

**3. Explore specific reading and language areas,** such as the eight presented in Part Three, when there are questions about your child's progress:

- ATTITUDE, INCENTIVE, BEHAVIOR: Influences on Learning to Read
- ORGANIZATION: Organizing, Planning, Completing Work
- THE ALPHABET: Letter-Sound Understanding, Alphabet Recognition, Reversals
- WORD RECOGNITION: Context, Memory, Letter-Sounds, Word-Parts
- WORD MEANING: Understanding Words While Listening, Speaking, Reading, and Writing
- COMPREHENSION: Understanding What One Reads
- ORAL/SILENT READING: Mechanics of Reading Out Loud and Silently
- WRITING AND DRAWING: Forming Letters and Pictures

Do any of these eight areas appear to be more of a concern than others?

**4. Identify behaviors which are signs of strength or need.** I offer a list of observations beginning in Part Three for each of the eight reading-language areas listed above. Mark your observations in this book or use the "Reading Log" suggested in Part Two to make notes on observations which apply to your child. You will see that certain behaviors overlap into various reading and language categories.

**5. Involve your child in identifying significant behavior.** Don't show your child what you have marked or noted from your observations. Just read over the observations as listed and discuss one or two of

**5. Involve your child** *(continued)*
the eight areas at a time. Too much at once will be overwhelming. Which observations appear to cause your child to say, "That's me." Some children know themselves far better than we realize. Others refuse to admit or fail to see how they act.

Regardless of your child's reaction, I have found that these observation guidelines open the door for communication with a child. I have witnessed amazing results when *students know* what certain behaviors are telling us. Many students have accepted more responsibility for their learning because they know what they are doing and what they might do to improve.

**6. Talk with your child's teacher**. Ask the teacher's opinion about the observations you and your child have made. You may be expecting more or less than your child is ready to do at a certain age or stage of development. Together with your child's teacher you may begin to see a pattern in the observation lists. You have probably marked more observations in one area than in another. Any of the eight areas in which few observations have been marked are possible strong points. Those categories in which many observations have been marked are areas of need. There is no magical number that determines strong areas or areas of need. Numbers will vary among different children. I have found that the guidelines I have just described have worked best for me.

**7. Set goals based on your child's strengths and needs**. By knowing your child's strengths and needs, you will spend your time more wisely when trying to help with assignments or with just applying reading in daily life. Emphasize your child's strong areas when encountering something relatively new. Then recognize that your child may show signs of frustration when required to do assignments that stress areas of greatest need. When needing to do an assignment which will cause sure frustration, see some of the suggestions offered under "Influences on Learning to Read".

**8. Try a few activities at a time**. With each set of observations, you will find recommended activities. Don't try to improve everything at once. Use the Reading Log or something similar to record the activities which work best, and those which do not seem to work. Remember: parent, child, and teacher should be involved. I am suggesting activities which I have seen work best, but not every

**8. Try a few at a time** *(continued)*
activity is appropriate for every child. You may find that the school is doing some of the activities which are suggested. You may be asked to try some things to supplement what is currently being done at school.

**9. Change goals and activities periodically**. Change may be necessary because certain activities have worked and goals have been met. We also need to alter our plans when things aren't working. Don't expect change overnight. You will need to *be consistent and positive* in your efforts.

After talking with the teacher and trying a set of activities for over a month or two, try a different approach. *Don't change too much at once*. If you throw out four or five ideas at once and start all new ones, you will not be able to narrow down what works best.

**10. Keep communicating**! Let everyone involved, especially your child, know when even the slightest improvement is seen. Nothing succeeds like success!

This is not a magical formula, but I have seen these ideas work when parents, teachers and children become involved. These members of The Reading Triangle need to stay involved over a period of time. Stick with it.

# Part Two

## THE READING LOG

THE READING LOG is an effective way to keep a record of a child's progress. I am providing a sample log sheet, shown on the next page, to help you get a start. I would suggest that you use the same log format in a separate notebook. Record your observations and subsequent activities there. Whether you use the log or not, find some way of recording observations and activities. You and your child need to see even the slightest evidence of success.

I realize that it takes time to write in a log, but it is so rewarding to have a personalized record of progress rather than a checklist or list of grades. Write in it as often as you can. Sometimes you may write weekly, at other times, once a month. Try to write at least every six months, so you can begin to see a pattern of growth in reading.

**The Reading Log — A Sample**

- Record observations.
- Tell how well the activities you tried worked.
- Occasionally, add your child's observations.

Jane's Reading Log

1/29 Jane read Curious George. She rarely stopped at periods and added words that didn't fit the story. She did use expression and tried to blend the sounds in words. When I asked her to tell me what she read, she had trouble getting things in the right order.

3/20 Jane read another Curious George story. She used good expression, blended the sounds in words, and stopped at periods. She could tell me the first part of the story. Jane still adds words that aren't there - but they're making more sense.

3/22 I asked Jane about how she thinks she reads out loud. She didn't believe that she added words that weren't there. She read three pages from her Curious George book on to the tape recorder... then she listened. As she looked at the story, she was amazed at how many words she added.

*Curious George,* H. A. Rey, Houghton Mifflin Co., Boston, 1941. Renewed 1961.

# Part Three

## READING OBSERVATIONS AND ACTIVITIES

PART ONE PROVIDES the guidelines necessary for applying the observation lists and activities in the following eight reading and language-related areas:

- ATTITUDE, INCENTIVE, BEHAVIOR
- ORGANIZATION
- THE ALPHABET
- WORD RECOGNITION
- WORD MEANING
- COMPREHENSION
- ORAL/SILENT READING
- WRITING AND DRAWING

I have personally used the observation lists and activities suggested when working with children of all ages. My graduate students have also used them while teaching elementary and secondary students. I have asked my graduate students to help me narrow down the most significant observations which helped them see the reading strengths and needs in their students. Then I asked them to help me list those activities which helped most, especially when offering suggestions to parents.

As I leave the following material in your hands, let me remind you that *our most important responsibility is to make reading a comfortable, meaningful, and enjoyable experience for each child.* DON'T STRESS ANY SPECIFIC SKILL to the point of sacrificing your child's love of reading.

# ATTITUDE, INCENTIVE, BEHAVIOR

## Influences on Learning to Read

**OBSERVATIONS**

Certain attitudes and behaviors can affect a child's performance in reading. The following list of observations may help parents, children, and teachers determine strengths and needs in this area. A child having difficulties in attitude, incentive, or behavior . . .

- ☐ Lacks positive attitude toward reading.
- ☐ Has a short attention span when listening or reading.
- ☐ Consistently says, "I don't know" when asked questions.
- ☐ Withdraws from a situation: pouting, leaving to do something else, changes the subject, diverts your attention from what should be done.
- ☐ Evidences a variety of behavior problems: may be critical of others, boasts about himself unrealistically, tries various methods to manipulate the situation, . . .

## Influences on Learning to Read

**Observations** (*continued*)

- ☐ Shows signs of frustration: head is down a great deal, little eye contact with materials or person with whom he is speaking, increasing level of activity (squirms, plays with objects, pulls at hair, rubs hands and face a great deal . . .), work is completed very quickly but incorrectly . . .

- ☐ Tests limits of what is acceptable behavior, more so than most.

- ☐ Lacks desire or purpose: "Do I have to do this?" "Why do I have to learn this?" "This is dumb!"

- ☐ Tries to restructure what is planned; wants his own way all the time and is not willing to listen to directions from others.

- ☐ Has poor attendance at school: tardiness or absenteeism or similar signs of avoidance.

- ☐ Is not committed to consistent completion of a task.

# ATTITUDE, INCENTIVE, BEHAVIOR

### Influences on Learning to Read

## ACTIVITIES

1. **Your child must see adults read** . . . newspapers, directions on medicine bottles, recipes, advertisements, traffic signs. Read these out loud so your child sees and hears the relevance and importance of knowing how to read.

2. **Encourage your child.** Having done a task well or achieved a goal, no matter how small and insignificant it may seem, praise your child. Display work (provide a special scrapbook for older students who shy away from having their work prominently displayed). Write notes which tell your child something positive. Enclose the notes as surprises in lunch boxes, on a pillow before bedtime, and in other special places. Such notes are great motivators for reading.

3. **Take time to go over the good work** your child has done, instead of only spending time on poor-quality work. Give tangible signs that work has been done well: hugs, a kind word to others in your child's presence. I said a "tangible sign," not a material reward. Such material rewards as candy and toys may work now and then, but they do not have the lasting effect that other signs which you can give may have.

4. **Keep communication open between home and school**, so you, your child, and the teacher are working together to meet similar, realistic goals.

5. **Learn the most appropriate level of material for your child** to succeed in reading. Ask your child's teacher to recommend appropriate material or please see Activity 1 under *Oral Reading*. In most cases, reading materials to be read at home should be at an easier level than those in which your child is instructed

## Influences on Learning to Read

**Activities** (*continued*)

at school. Your child needs to read the material at home independently, and in school your child is still learning what is needed to achieve more difficult material. If your child must read books which are beyond a suggested reading level or wants to do so, you can read to your child before the material is read independently. Most children will understand what they hear much better than what they will read on their own. Hearing it first will get your child ready to read the material later.

6. **Set goals and define a reasonable time limit for working.** Have your child become involved in setting goals and time limits. Use a timer, if necessary, to help gauge study time . . . 15-20 minute intervals or more as your child gets older. Don't allow intrusions on that time.

7. **Try to make learning exciting, interesting, and relevant to everyday living.** Take advantage of commercial or student-made games designed to teach reading and language. As a natural extension of daily life, help your child see that reading is everywhere. Ask that your child take phone messages; read billboards and road signs; write and read the grocery list; read junk mail and determine its importance; read the T.V./movie guide . . .

8. **Help family members understand your child's needs** in reading and how things are progressing. Converse regularly with your child about what is happening with regard to your child's reading improvement. We can't help unless your child wants to improve and knows how.

9. **Ask for special help from your child's school.** Your child's teacher, a reading specialist, speech and language pathologist, social worker, psychologist, school nurse, counselor and other professionals are available through most public schools. Ask for help.

10. **A complete physical examination should be done if problems persist.** Thoroughly check vision, hearing, and other physical factors which can affect learning.

# ORGANIZATION

## Organizing, Planning, Completing Work

**OBSERVATIONS**
Organization is important if a child is to succeed in developing the complexities involved in reading and writing. A child having difficulties with organization . . .

- ☐ Has problems making decisions or establishing priorities of what should be done.
- ☐ Shows evidence of messy papers, desks, drawers . . . Never puts things away.
- ☐ Does not complete assigned tasks.
- ☐ Loses papers, crayons, books . . . Is constantly losing things.
- ☐ Starts at bottom and goes to top when writing, or is not going left-to-right.
- ☐ Crowds or does not properly use spaces in writing.
- ☐ Skips sections of a worksheet or test without noticing. (Make sure this is not a problem with vision.)

## Organization

**Observations** (*continued*)

- ☐ Has difficulty sorting objects or words into logical order.

- ☐ Has difficulty following more than one direction at a time. Always asking, "What?" (Make sure this is not related to a hearing problem.)

- ☐ Looks around a great deal and is disturbed by the slightest sight or sound. Does not appear able to concentrate long enough to complete a task.

- ☐ May appear clumsy or accident prone. (This may be related to a visual-motor problem.)

- ☐ Does not pace oneself well. Works too slowly or too quickly for the task.

# ORGANIZATION

## Organizing, Planning, Completing Work

### ACTIVITIES

1. **Limit the amount of work to be completed and gradually increase the amount** with each assignment if your child has difficulty completing lengthy assignments. Or have your child complete only a portion by a designated time and then show the work to someone to see how things are progressing. By breaking the assignment down, it may not seem as overwhelming.

2. **Write out a plan that shows the sequence that should be followed** in doing a task. Your child may need to see, as well as hear, what needs to be done. You could use color-coding as signals of where to begin and stop — green meaning to start in a certain place and red telling the child where to stop.

3. **Discuss a task before it is begun.** Ask, "How do you know when you will be finished?" Help your child see, before an assignment or task begins, what signals to look for to know the work is finished: time limits, skills to be achieved, number of problems to do . . . This helps your child recognize or sense a goal that needs to be met.

4. **Ask your child to repeat what is to be done** once directions have been given.

5. **Make expectations reasonable and clear**, so you can avoid messy desks, drawers . . . Don't assume your child knows what is expected. Your child may need more specific guidance.

## Organization

**Activities** (*continued*)

6. **PRAISE YOUR CHILD when goals have been met.** Also give praise when your child has accomplished some of the steps that will eventually help reach designated goals.

7. **Help guide and show your child how a task can be organized.** Don't assume your child knows.

8. **Set a good example.** Try to show how to organize things — clothes in a drawer, papers in a notebook, books on a shelf, etc. Provide a place to organize and store things.

9. **Set goals with your child.** This could be in the form of a brief contract or just a two-way discussion in which your child makes some commitment to strive to meet goals.

10. **Help your child develop responsibilities for completing tasks by questioning rather than telling** what to do. Example: "What homework do you have? How do you know when you have finished it correctly?"

11. **Encourage your child to write lists** or notes to remember things. These don't have to be long sentences or phrases. Single-word reminders are good for a start. Check off as they are completed.

# THE ALPHABET

## Letter-Sound Understanding, Alphabet Recognition, and Reversals

### OBSERVATIONS

Some children have difficulty understanding how letters or symbols can represent sounds in words. Some have difficulty remembering the names of letters. It is important to recognize that *some children will learn words and can read stories without having learned letter-sounds or the names of the letters*.

They may learn to use context or they may memorize words. When words cannot be read using context or memory, letter-sound understanding can help. Most children before the age of five or six will not independently apply letter-sound understanding when unlocking words.

A five or six year old who has been introduced to the alphabet and letter-sounds may be showing signs of difficulty if that child . . .

- ☐ Does not recognize or recall the sound represented by a letter.

- ☐ Can tell the letter-sound in a word when it is heard, but has difficulty applying that knowledge when the word is seen.

## The Alphabet

**Observations** (*continued*)

- ☐ Doesn't know the difference between a letter and a word; and a word and a sentence.
- ☐ Doesn't remember how to make the letters. Consistently asks, "How do I make that letter?"
- ☐ Does not recognize capitals or lower-case letters.

Some letters and words are reversed by children. A child who has difficulty with reversals . . .

- ☐ Starts to write from the wrong side of the paper or starts at the bottom and writes up the page.
- ☐ Turns letters and words around when seeing or when writing them. Makes the reversal errors more frequently when the letters or words need to be recalled from memory when writing, as compared to copying them.
- ☐ Has difficulty identifying left and right side of body after child is six or seven years of age.

# THE ALPHABET

## Letter-Sound Understanding, Alphabet Recognition, and Reversals

### ACTIVITIES

### A. Letter-Sound Understanding

1. **Help your child associate letter-sounds to a key word.** The key word should help your child remember the letter-sounds which give trouble. Ask your child or the teacher about key words which may be used at school, so you can reinforce them at home. When your child encounters a word and does not appear to recognize its letter-sound, ask your child to think of the key word which begins or contains that letter-sound. It is best if your child chooses meaningful key words, so the letter-sounds will be remembered more easily. Be aware that the following letters can be confusing, so check with your child's teacher to see how they are introduced in school and when: *c,g,x,a,e,i,o,u,y*.

2. **Remember that letters have names, and the letters represent sounds.** Try not to confuse your child by asking for the name of the letter when you really want the sound represented by the letter. Try not to ask for an isolated sound, "What does a *b* say?" Do ask for a key word that contains a particular letter-sound, "Can you think of a word that has a *b* at the beginning?"

3. **Children will often need help blending letter-sounds** in a sequence to form meaningful words. They may not automatically learn the letter-sounds and then say the word. See further suggestions in this area under *Word Recognition*.

**The Alphabet**

**Activities** (*continued*)

4. **Read poems, nursery rhymes, and other rhyming lines (music).** You will begin to show your child that words have rhythm and can have matching sounds.

5. **Try the Language Experience Approach** if your child needs to see the relationship between letters, words, sentences. Your child dictates a story and watches as you write. A child may copy or trace-over what you have written, and illustrate the story. Discuss letters, words, and sentences as you write.

**B. Alphabet Recognition**: You will need to make a set of upper-case (capital) and lower-case letters for the following activities. Notice that I did not say "small" letters. Lower-case letters are short and tall. Some children are confused by the comparative sizes. For example, a lower-case *h* may be as tall as an upper-case or capital *H*. Don't feel you are "talking over your child's head" by using the correct terms.

1. **Alphabet Book**: This helps children learn in sequence (A to Z). It also encourages them to associate a beginning sound with the letter. Take 26 sheets of paper, plus paper for a front and back cover. Have your child copy a capital and lower-case letter at the top of each page. You can add another way of helping your child remember the letters by having the letters drawn with a crayon on a bumpy surface — such as a window screen placed between the writing paper and the table. Thus, your child will be able to see, feel and say the letters. Then choose one or two letters a day and draw or cut out favorite pictures that are reminders of the sound that a particular letter represents at the beginning of a word. Have your child begin with consonants. The consonants are all the letters except *a, e, i,o,* and *u*. Usually the "hard-c" as in *cow* and the "hard-g" as in *goat* are introduced before the soft sounds as heard in *cent* or *giraffe*.

## The Alphabet

### Activities (*continued*)

2. **Matching Capital and Lower-Case Letters**: Use only 5 or 6 pair of upper and lower-case letters. Place the 5 or 6 pair face-up in random order on the table. Have your child see how quickly the capital and lower-case letters can be matched. Record the time it takes to make all the matches. Try to beat that time the next time your child does this activity. You can also increase the number of pairs.

3. **Alpha Sheet Matching**: Make a Bingo-type sheet with 25 boxes or 5 rows of blank squares and 5 columns of blank squares. Each player randomly fills in each square with capitals and lower-case letters. Choose letters which your child needs to practice recognizing. Using the upper-case and/or lower-case letter *cards* suggested for all of the alphabet activities, place the letter-cards in random order face down or put them in a box. Choose one letter at a time. Your child should name the letter which is to be matched on the "alpha sheet." You should show the child the letter-card to be matched if you want to stress matching, but you may just want to say the letter on the card if you are emphasizing your child's need to remember what specific letters look like without seeing the letters first. A winner is decided as in Bingo.

4. **Concentration**: This will help develop visual-memory and matching skills in addition to learning the names of the letters. Use about 6 pair of capital and lower-case letters at first. Turn the letters face-down in a 2 by 6 grid, 2 across and 6 in each column. The grid is a helpful way to have your child organize and remember the names of the letters. Have your child turn over two cards at a time — one from the left column where you may have placed all lower-case letters and one from the right column where you could place all capitals. If the capital and lower-case letters do not match, turn them face-down again. Try two others, saying the letters as they are turned over. See how quickly the child can match capitals to lower-case letters.

## The Alphabet

### Activities (*continued*)

### C. Reversals

1. **Keep samples of correct forms of letters near** for your child to use as he or she practices writing letters until the reversal is corrected. When your child is able to read or write the letters or words without reversing, reward your child by saying, "I don't think you need this letter on your desk or wall anymore." By placing the letter near for your child to copy correctly, you are providing the opportunity for your child to see the letter correctly rather than guess incorrectly. The more your child writes it incorrectly from memory, the more the reversal problem will remain.

2. **When you see a letter that your child often reverses, call it to your child's attention** without disrupting the train of thought while reading. This is another way of having your child see the proper way a letter looks.

3. **Show how a capital *B* and lower-case *b* can be compared.** They both face the same direction when written correctly. The lower-case *b* can be made into a capital *B* by adding a bump on the top. Try to think of other, similar clues to help your child associate, and remember how to make other letters and words which cause difficulty.

4. **See the Spelling Dictionary activity** under *Word Recognition*, Activity 11.

# WORD RECOGNITION

## OBSERVATIONS

Words are usually recognized by using one or a combination of three approaches: context, memory, and/or letter-sounds and word-parts. A child who has difficulty with word recognition . . .

- ☐ Does not use context or meaningful surroundings as clues for recognizing a word.
- ☐ Looks too quickly at the word, guessing and not taking the time to really "see" it.
- ☐ Confuses common "sight words:" there-where, then-when . . .
- ☐ Begins to "sound-out" or decode a word but guesses at the ending.
- ☐ Says a consonant blend at the beginning of a word when there isn't one there (frame for fame, . . .) or does not recognize and blend blends when they are in a word.
- ☐ Has difficulty with consonant digraphs: shoe, chin, thumb, wheel, phone . . .

## Word Recognition

**Observations** (*continued*)

☐ Confuses long and short vowel sounds: long vowels-acorn, eagle, ice, open, united; short vowels-apple, elephant, Indian, ostrich, umbrella.

☐ Doesn't know other vowel patterns besides those which are long and short: saw, cow, moon, boy . . .

☐ Cannot blend letter-sounds in sequence.

☐ Attempts to sound-out or decode all words or all the letters in words even if words cannot be analyzed in that manner. Fails to recognize the need to use context and/or memory.

☐ Tries to use phonics "rules" which cannot be used on all words.

☐ Has difficulty with prefixes, suffixes, syllables, and other word-parts.

# WORD RECOGNITION

## ACTIVITIES

1. **Expose your child to words in a variety of ways.** Encourage your child to hear, feel, write and not just see words.

2. **Keep a list of commonly confused words to use in different games.** Example: Concentration Game: Choose 5 or 6 troublesome words. Write the same word on two different cards, so you have 5 or 6 pair of words. You may increase this number as your child becomes more proficient. Turn cards face-down in rows and columns. Your child should turn only two cards over at a time and read each word revealed. Keep those that match. See how long it takes your child to match and read all the words. Record how long it takes to make all the matches. Encourage your child to beat that time the next time you play, or add more words to make it more challenging.

3. **To improve the use of context clues, scramble and unscramble sentences.** If your child has difficulty with this at first, have your child read the sentence aloud before it is scrambled. As your child gets better, new words should be added to original sentences to see if your child can figure out where the new word meaningfully fits.

4. **Use meaning to help sound-out and read words.** For example, in the sentence, "The dog ran down the street," your child may not know *street*. Ask your child to think of a word which begins with the *str* letter combination which meaningfully fits into the sentence.

5. **Context and sounding-out**: Leave words out of stories. Ask your child to fill in a meaningful word which begins with a designated letter-sound (combination). Example: "Ben Hur was determined to win the ch____race."

## Word Recognition

**Activities** (*continued*)

6. **Word Speed Up**: Take words from (1) readers, (2) sight word lists, and (3) best of all from those your child, you and the teacher have collected which have caused problems. Use a gameboard (sheet of paper or light card stock) divided into six equally-sized spaces, possibly three boxes at the top of the paper and three at the bottom. Number each space from 1 through 6. Use about 20 or more words and deal them face-down onto each of the six spaces. Try putting approximately the same number of words on each space. Your child is to work against the clock. Even when your child plays with other children, have them all work together to beat the clock, not each other. Set a time limit to see how long it should take to uncover and empty as many number-spaces as possible. Throw one die (from a pair of dice). The leader will quickly turn over the words on the space that matches the number on the die. Have the child read the words. If a word is correct, the child can keep it. If the word is not correct, the leader must read the word correctly and replace it face-down on the numbered space. See how many spaces are emptied before time is up. Do it again and try to reveal more number-spaces.

7. **Left-to-Right Blending**: Write a problem-word on a large card, about the size of a legal envelope. Place each word in a book or folder and gradually pull it out, so your child can read the word from left-to-right. If your child is working on certain letter-sounds, reveal the word sound by sound. If your child is working on syllables, reveal the word by syllables. When the entire word is revealed, be sure the sounds and syllables have been blended smoothly to form a meaningful word. If your child tends to guess at endings after seeing the beginning and fails to look carefully at the word, do not allow anything to be said until the entire word is revealed. Just have the child "mouth" the letter-sound combinations as they are shown and only say the word out loud when the full word is revealed. You may also ask your child to write the word as you reveal each sound or syllable. The child can see when the whole word is shown what the correct spelling should be. In the meantime, you are providing an opportunity to see how your child may be spelling other words which have similar beginning letter-sounds.

## Word Recognition

**Activities** (*continued*)

8. **Key Word Charts**: Make a key word chart for the letter-sounds which need to be reviewed and reinforced. These should include those your child is learning in school — single consonants, blends, digraphs, vowels . . . Have your child choose one key word which is a reminder of the letter-sound to be recalled. When your child encounters a word with the bothersome sound, ask your child to think of the key word with that letter-sound combination. This key word chart can also help show the various spellings which represent one sound. Example: Key Word for Long "a" could be *acorn*, but the long "a" sound can be spelled as in *aim, frame, neigh, tray*. As your child sees or needs to write words with various spellings for the same letter-sound, write the word using the correct spelling combination and point it out on the chart to your child. When your child asks to spell a word such as *weigh*, you can say, "It has the vowel sound as in *acorn*, but is spelled with the letter pattern as in *neigh*."

9. **Many commercial games** stress word recognition skills — Word Yahtzee, Scrabble . . . Explore toy departments and educational supply stores for many examples of word games.

10. **Very few so-called phonic rules apply** in the majority of word-recognition situations. Help your child recognize words through context, memory, and sometimes through other means. Let your child know there are some generalizations which usually or sometimes apply, but *avoid* relying on rules to unlock words.

11. **Make a Spelling Dictionary**. This dictionary idea works well for adults as well as for children. Words are usually misspelled over and over again because we make a stab at them or we tell our child, "Try to spell it by the way it sounds." The word is then written incorrectly and has to be corrected. *First impressions usually last the longest*. So the more we try, but misspell, the more we become accustomed to the misspelling and aggravate the problem. We need to see the words correctly as much as possible before we commit those words to writing.

## Word Recognition

**Activities** (*continued*)

**11. Make a Spelling Dictionary** (*continued*)

Purchase or make a small booklet with at least 26 pages. Have your child write the letters alphabetically, one per page. Start by having a brainstorming session in which you and your child name as many bothersome words as possible. You may ask your child's teacher for suggestions also. Write the words correctly into the Spelling Dictionary as your child watches. If you write the words on a separate paper and have your child copy them into the dictionary, be sure they have been copied correctly. After the first session, encourage your child to carry the dictionary in school or wherever it may be needed when writing. As your child discovers new problem words, add them to the dictionary. I have seen the Spelling Dictionary work effectively for children from first grade up. Adults can jot the bothersome words in the back of a pocket calendar or address book, so the correct spellings will always be within reach.

# WORD MEANING

## Listening, Speaking, Reading, Writing

**OBSERVATIONS**

Understanding spoken language is related to understanding written words as one reads. A child having difficulty with word meaning . . .

- ☐ Tends to repeat familiar vocabulary and not use new words after they are introduced.
- ☐ Appears to know what the name of something is but has trouble recalling it quickly in order to say it, use it in conversation, or write it.
- ☐ Has difficulty being specific in defining or describing words.
- ☐ Has difficulty varying the pattern or style of a sentence when speaking or writing: "I like dogs. I like to play ball . . ."
- ☐ Says "I don't know" frequently when asked for ideas or thoughts on a subject.

## Word Meaning

**Observations** (*continued*)

- ☐ Has difficulty understanding that words can have more than one meaning: "The boy *rose* from the bed." *Rose* is not always a flower.

- ☐ Fails to use the meaning of a sentence or familiar surroundings to determine an unknown word. Is not using context.

- ☐ Does not talk or write in complete sentences. May show reluctance to talk at all.

- ☐ Has trouble determining broad categories before becoming specific or has difficulty taking specifics and giving them a broad category. "This vegetable is a carrot." (Broad to Specific) "This carrot is a vegetable." (Specific to Broad)

# WORD MEANING

## Listening, Speaking, Reading, Writing

### ACTIVITIES

1. **Deal with words which are relevant and important in the environment** when attempting to improve your child's understanding of words: food labels, medical warnings, street signs, danger signs, business signs . . . Take trips to the zoo, circus . . . and talk about what you see.

2. **Read to your child regularly**. Your child needs to hear meaningful words. Read anything — letters, articles, signs, billboards, poems, music lyrics, cereal box labels, recipes, car names, ads, or books. As you read, occasionally stop before the end of the sentence and have your child complete the thought. Don't criticize if the words your child uses differ from the author's. If your child says something that fits the meaning of the sentence, praise the effort. Discuss the similarities and differences between what your child said and what the author wrote.

3. **Play commercial or T.V. games** relating to word meanings or categorization: Twenty-Questions, Jeopardy, Scrabble, Scribbage, Twenty-Five Thousand Dollar Pyramid . . .

4. **Have your child hide a picture or object** in a paper sack. Ask your child to write or tell everything about the object except what it is. Have others try to draw it from the description. You may just want others to guess what the object is after your child gives the description.

## Word Meaning

**Activities** (*continued*)

5. **Ask your child to name things** along the roadsides that fit into certain categories when your family takes a trip. Compete to see who in the family can get the most in a given category: animals, plants, places . . .

6. **Talk with your child**. Children need to participate in conversation.

7. **Encourage your child to express feelings in words** . . . not always through actions.

8. **Encourage your child to keep a diary or log** of daily or special activities. This provides relevant experiences with writing and using words.

9. **Ask your librarian** for books that do fun things with words . . . idioms, figures of speech, similes. For example, be sure to see Fred Gwynne's book, *Chocolate Moose for Dinner* (Publisher: Dutton, New York, 1976).

10. **Have your child give directions** for making or doing something. Another person is to follow the directions very literally and see what final results are achieved. How do the results compare to what your child intended?

11. **Vocabulary Bingo**. Words are arranged on a Bingo board using approximately 20 to 25 blank boxes arranged in four or five rows of five each. Fill in each box with a word from a list your child needs to learn. Someone who leads will read definitions. Your child will cover the word that matches the definition. The winner is determined in the same way as in Bingo.

# COMPREHENSION

## Listening, Reading

**OBSERVATIONS**

A child who is having difficulty understanding what is read . . .

- ☐ Can't recall story content, has a poor memory.
- ☐ Puts in own words while reading out loud to the point that the meaning of the story is lost.
- ☐ Has difficulty organizing ideas in order to retell story.
- ☐ Has difficulty predicting what the story will be about or how a story may end.
- ☐ Has difficulty inferring what the author means, or has difficulty reading between the lines.
- ☐ Does not use context to understand words.
- ☐ Is reluctant to express opinions about the story.
- ☐ Fails to pay attention to details in a story: color, shapes, numbers . . .
- ☐ Has a blank look as though not understanding when listening to a story.

# COMPREHENSION

## Listening, Reading

### ACTIVITIES

1. **Experience is the greatest aid to comprehension**. Understanding comes best when your child can somehow experience what is to be encountered in a story. If your child is to read about a winter carnival, and you live in a climate which has snowy winters, your child will be able to relate more easily to the story-content. When children are to read what they have not personally experienced, we need to provide experiences, or we can help them pretend what it would be like. Don't wait until your child is about to read a story, however, to share experiences. If you take advantage of talking and sharing new experiences with your youngster regularly, your child will be able to understand more of what is read because of the experiences you have provided.

2. **Your child must READ, READ, READ**. Encourage your child to read materials that are interesting. The materials should be at a level appropriate for success. Talk with your child's teacher about the best types of materials for your child or see Activity 1 under *Oral Reading* activities.

3. **Find alternative ways for your child to share** what has been read. Have your child impersonate a favorite character in the book, make up a puppet show or a play . . . Have fun with reading.

4. **Set purposes before reading begins**. It may sometimes help to read the questions that come at the end of the story to know what to look for as one reads.

## Comprehension

### Activities (*continued*)

5. **Pre-read** before reading out loud. Read silently first. Encourage your child to ask about words which may cause difficulty when reading out loud.

6. **Make predictions** based on picture clues, the title, or topics within the story. Have your child ask two or three questions which might be answered at the end of the story. If your child has difficulty thinking of questions, provide some choices. Give your child samples of types of questions which might be asked. Have your child choose those most likely to appear at the end of the story, based on a quick overview of the story.

7. **Main idea**: Use newspaper articles, cut headlines off, and have your child listen to or read the article. Then write a headline. Compare the headline your child wrote or suggested to that printed by the newspaper. Does your child's headline capture the main idea of the article? Discuss with your child.

8. **Question your child** as a means of guidance in searching out the necessary details in a story. Don't tell where to find the details.

9. **Cut out a series of cartoon or comic strips**. Put the pictures in order. Write or tell a story to go with the pictures.

10. **Use the tape recorder**. Have your child listen to stories or subject matter which others have tape-recorded. If the story is too difficult or the subject matter too hard to be read independently, your child will benefit by hearing the material first. This can be done without the tape recorder, of course, if you sit down and read to your child in person.

11. **Short stories are essential** for reluctant readers.

# ORAL READING/SILENT READING

## OBSERVATIONS

**A. Oral Reading**: Individuals having difficulties with reading out loud . . .

- ☐ Do not use punctuation clues as they read. They make sentences run together or stop in the middle of sentences where there are no punctuation marks.
- ☐ Add words that aren't there.
- ☐ Substitute words that don't make sense, possibly relying on the shape of the words or the letter-sounds rather than the meaning of the sentence.
- ☐ Omit words.
- ☐ Read in a voice that is distinctly different from a conversational tone.
- ☐ Repeat words or phrases frequently.

## Oral Reading/Silent Reading

### Observations (*continued*)

**B. Silent Reading:** A child having difficulty when reading silently . . .

- ☐ Uses his fingers excessively pointing to each word to keep his place. This may be necessary at first, but should eventually stop (about the third grade or eight years of age). Your child's hand may continue to be a general guide, not a pointer.
- ☐ Loses place easily, whether or not the hand is used to guide.
- ☐ Softly whispers and moves lips when reading. This tends to slow the reader down considerably.
- ☐ Tends to look away frequently and has difficulty concentrating.

# ORAL READING/SILENT READING

## ACTIVITIES

### A. Oral Reading

1. **Be sure your child is reading at a level that will allow success.** Consult with your child's teacher, but there is another way you can generally tell if a story is too hard. It has been called, "The Rule of Thumb." Have your child read the first page of a book. As your child encounters a word that cannot be figured out easily, one finger is put down for each difficult word — beginning with the small finger. If all five fingers are down by the end of the page, the book may be too hard to be read independently.

2. **Read materials that were meant to be shared out loud**: plays, news, letters from friends and relatives, poems, stories a child has written, limericks, jokes, music lyrics . . .

3. **Use the tape recorder**. Have your child read the story or other material to be shared out loud onto the tape recorder. Many children do not realize that they are omitting words, substituting words, not stopping at periods, reading in a monotone, adding meaningless words . . . As you and your child listen to what has been recorded, help your child determine what oral reading techniques are needed to improve.

4. **Pick out conversation** in a story and read only that.

5. **Pick a partner**. Read to a friend. Don't read out loud just to be reading out loud. Your child should be sharing something with a friend or with someone who is willing to listen and discuss what has been read.

## Oral Reading/Silent Reading

**Activities** *(continued)*

6. **Listen to stories.** Look for records or tapes that go with books. Your child can hear someone read with expression and imitate the style needed when reading out loud.

7. **Use Language Experience** stories to relate your child's language to reading. Encourage your child to read the story after you have written what has been dictated.

**B. Silent Reading:**

1. **Have your child's vision thoroughly checked** to be sure that reading is comfortable. When children turn away or lose their place easily, they may be experiencing vision trouble. Watch for other signs of discomfort that may be clues telling you there may be a problem with vision.

2. **To help your child rely less on word-by-word pointing,** place a bookmark or other marker, such as one hand above the words and move down the page. By placing the marker above the words, your child will no longer block out sentences as the eyes move down the page. Many forget about needing a marker. (This activity should not be necessary until about the third grade or above. Before that, children need to have a means of pointing or keeping their place, as they are at the beginning stages of reading.)

3. **Whispering softly or moving lips may be your child's way of continuing oral reading** even though silent reading is expected. Some of us who understand and remember more of what we hear may rely on such whispering to help gain more meaning even though it slows us down. Others, primarily above third grade, who can learn best without whispering can try to break the habit by gently placing a finger on their lips as they read. This will help children become aware that the lips are moving. As the finger is gently pressed against the lips, it can help stop the lip movement.

# WRITING AND DRAWING

**OBSERVATIONS**

Writing and drawing are important language-related experiences. Our goal should be to encourage our children to share their creative ideas through writing and drawing. They may be frustrated in their efforts to reach that goal, however, because they are having difficulty with the mechanics of writing or drawing. A child having difficulties in these areas . . .

- ☐ Holds pencil or crayon awkwardly.
- ☐ Has difficulty coloring within designated boundaries.
- ☐ Has difficulty forming letters correctly in either manuscript (printing) or cursive (writing).
- ☐ Cannot manipulate scissors easily when cutting.
- ☐ Spaces letters and words improperly, and has difficulty placing letters and words consistently on the lines when writing.
- ☐ Has difficulty in physical activities such as hopping, skipping, jumping.
- ☐ Lacks left-to-right organization. May start writing from the wrong side of the paper.
- ☐ Has more difficulty copying from a distance than copying at a close-range. (Be sure this is not a problem with vision.)

# WRITING AND DRAWING

## ACTIVITIES

1. **Your child must see the correct form of a letter** by watching someone write it. Your child may need to trace over, copy at a close-range, or do some of both before achieving success in copying letters and words from a distance or on one's own.

2. **Place a correct sample of letters, numbers, or words** which cause your child difficulty in some location near the writing table. Take the sample away once your child thinks and shows evidence of not having difficulty forming the designated letters, numbers, or words.

3. **Limit goals** for improving writing to those letters or words which can be improved quickly at first, then increase goals as short-range ones are met.

4. **Print a word which causes difficulty** on a large strip of paper. Have your child cut it, scramble, unscramble, then copy and read the word. (Cutting, left-to-right organization, writing . . . are all included.)

5. **Give your child color codes** or verbal directions to show where to begin and where to stop. For example, draw a green dot on the left margin. Green means *go* so the child will know to start on the left, not the right. Put a red dot at the right margin. Ask questions before your child begins to write, "Where are you going to start? What direction will you go? What does each red dot mean? Where do you go when you finish writing on this line?"

## Writing and Drawing

**Activities** (*continued*)

6. **Experiment with different sizes** of pencils and paper with different sized spaces between the lines. See which produces the most comfortable writing for your child.

7. **Language Experience Stories**: By watching as someone writes what is dictated, your child can see how letters, words, and sentences are created. When your child is ready, encourage tracing, copying, or writing stories independently. This approach helps bridge a gap between what may be considered the mechanics of writing or drawing and *creativity – the ultimate goal*.

# SUMMARY: SECTION TWO

## PUTTING THE READING TRIANGLE TO WORK

SECTION TWO provides guidelines and activities for you, your child, and your child's teacher. The suggestions are offered to help a school-age child, kindergarten and older, succeed in reading.

**Part One** presents ten Guidelines for Communication. These guidelines are designed to help the parent, child, and teacher become more informed about a child's strengths and needs in reading and language. With that information, I believe you have a basis for better communication between home and school about what may be best to help your child improve in reading. Better communication between home and school should mean that everyone involved in helping your child will be aiming at similar goals — not going off in different directions.

**Part Two** suggests the use of a Reading Log. The log or any similar, informal recording method will help you, your child, and the teacher begin to see progress. You do not have to use the Reading Log I suggest — but DO use some means of recording what works and does not work best for your child.

**Part Three** offers specific observation checklists and suggested activities in eight reading and language areas. Watch your youngster perform on daily home and school activities. No formal testing is necessary to mark the observation checklists. As you observe your child, you will begin to see a pattern of strengths and needs in certain reading and language areas. Be sure to discuss these with your child's teacher. You want to be sure you are not expecting more than your child is ready to do at a certain age or stage of development.

Activities are then suggested in eight reading and language areas. These activities have succeeded in helping students with whom I have worked. The best guarantees for success, however, are (1) to keep your child actively involved in knowing what is needed for improvement, and (2) to keep communication open between home and school.

Remember that our most important responsibility with regard to reading should be to make reading a comfortable, meaningful, and enjoyable experience for each child. Don't stress any specific skill to the point of sacrificing your child's enjoyment of reading.

# SOME CLOSING THOUGHTS

IN THIS BOOK, I have shared information and ideas which I trust will help you as you guide your child toward successful, enjoyable reading experiences. In the following pages, I have included additional reference information to help you gather more ideas or clarify those I have presented.

In the list of *Further Information and Ideas for Parents* are suggestions of where you can get further information about what you can do to help your child with reading. Finally a *Glossary* is included which gives the meanings of many reading and language terms. Teachers use these terms, and I have used many in this book. I hope the glossary will help you better understand what educators are talking about!

# Further Information and Ideas for Parents

HERE ARE SOME suggestions of where you can gather more information and ideas about reading. We have included the addresses of all publishers listed.

1. **Allyn and Bacon** (7 Wells Ave., Newton, MA 02159) offers a booklet entitled "Your Child's Reading—What You Can Do!" It gives tips on things that parents can do to improve their children's reading.

2. **Babies Need Books** (Atheneum, 597 Fifth Ave., New York, NY 10017) by Dorothy Butler is a thorough guide for parents. It deals with early childhood and the introduction of books to the very young.

3. **Questions Parents Ask About Reading** (Avanti Associates, 9 Marietta Lane, Mercerville, NJ 08619) by Dr. Nicholas P. Criscuolo offers brief, meaningful answers to questions about reading.

4. **A Parent's Guide to Children's Reading** (Bantam, 666 Fifth Ave., New York, NY 10019) by Nancy Larrick is in its fifth edition. She emphasizes the importance of reading in a child's life. An annotated list of "Books They Like" occupies much of the book. It is excellent!

5. **The Children's Book Council** (67 Irving Place, New York, NY 10003) is an association that encourages the reading of children's books. A brochure called "Choosing a Child's Book" offers guidance in choosing children's books and suggests sources of information about children, reading, and books.

6. **Choosing Books for Children: A Commonsense Guide** (Delacorte, 245 E. Forty-seventh St., New York, NY 10017) by Betsy Hearne is a helpful guide for parents who wish to know the what, when, and how of sharing books with children. It suggests books for the preschooler to the young adult.

7. **Your Child Can Read, and You Can Help** (Doubleday, 245 Park Ave., New York, NY 10017) by Dr. Jane Ervin offers an annotated list of children's books, organizations, and support services that are concerned with reading and learning problems. She gives parents a list of five book clubs and thirty-two sources for finding recommended books for children.

8. **Educational Supply Stores** appear to be teachers' stores, but parents are welcome. Ask your child's teacher or check the yellow pages under "Educational Supplies" to locate those in your area. You will find records, tapes, games, toys, books, activities, and ideas for parents. Talk with your child's teacher for recommendations of what will best meet your child's needs.

9. **Houghton-Mifflin Co.** (2 Park St., Boston, MA 02107) offers informative pamphlets for parents: "Your Child and Reading, How You Can Help"; "A Primer for Parents" by Paul Kee, introduced by Dr. William Durr; and "The What and Why of Beginning Reading" by Dr. William Hillerich.

10. **The International Reading Association** (800 Barksdale Rd., P.O. Box 8139, Newark, DE 19711) offers materials, seminars, books, journal articles, and conferences for parents. A list of reading materials to aid parents will be mailed on request.

11. **Public and school libraries** offer tremendous opportunities, yet we so often overlook them. You may check out books, tapes, records, films, filmstrips, and computer materials. Most libraries offer special programs (plays, crafts, workshops). Children can become involved with what they hear and see in books.

12. **Bucket-Aids** (M-R Publications, 6120 Gardenia, Lansing, MI 48910) includes seven publications developed by Mrs. Dinghy Sharp and others. In the late 1960s, Mrs. Sharp and a teaching colleague created a tutor training program called the Bucket Brigade. Through this program, parents and other volunteers are trained to help children from kindergarten through third grade. The "Bucket-Aids" include the following materials:

    - Bucket-Sounds—Dinghy Sharp
    - Bucket Math—Dinghy Sharp and Ruby Martin

- Beginning Reading Language Experience Approach—Dinghy Sharp and Audrey Schurgin
- Color-Code Script—Marie Littler and Dingy Sharp
- Color-Code Paper—Dinghy Sharp and Marie Littler
- Bucket Center—Dinghy Sharp
- Bucket Aids—Dinghy Sharp and Judy Haught

13. **The National Council of Teachers of English** (1111 Kenyon Rd., Urbana, IL 61801) offers materials such as the brochure "How to Help Your Child Become a Better Writer."

14. **Parents and Reading** (Northwest Regional Educational Laboratory, 300 S.W. Sixth Ave., Portland, OR 97204) is a program for parents. It was prepared by Dr. Roy Truby. The program includes a parent's booklet and an administrative manual. The parent's booklet offers information and suggestions for activities and books to share with children at home. The administrative manual is designed for administrators and teachers who want to plan a "Parents and Reading" program.

15. **Parents As Reading Partners** is a program initiated by New York State Senator James Donovan. In this program, parents are encouraged to read to children for fifteen minutes a day. For materials that describe this program, write to Sen. James Donovan, Room 708, Legislative Office Bldg., Albany, NY 12247.

16. **Parent's Choice** (Parent's Choice Foundation, Box 185, Waban, MA 92168) is a quarterly publication. It reviews children's media, books for parents and children, television, movies, and music. Each issue also contains a variety of articles.

17. **The Read-Aloud Handbook** (Penguin, 40 W. Twenty-third St., New York, NY 10010) by Jim Trelease offers practical ideas about reading aloud to children. He includes a list of more than 300 read-aloud books.

18. **Scholastic Inc.** (730 Broadway, New York, NY 10003) offers a nicely illustrated brochure called "Reading in the Home."

# READING GLOSSARY

**Accent**

The relative amount of breath-force with which a syllable is spoken. Example: FA' vor, im POR' tant.

**Auditory Discrimination**

The ability to tell the difference between sounds.

**Basal Reader**

One of a series of reading texts used as the basis for a school or classroom reading program — usually produced by the same publisher.

**Comprehension**

Understanding what is read.

**Configuration**

The shape of a word.

**Consonant**

A letter of the alphabet which is not a vowel or does not represent a vowel sound. The letters *y* and *w* are consonants when they represent the sounds as heard at the beginning of "year" and "we," but they become vowels when they help produce vowel sounds as in "happy, gym, sky, cow, saw."

**Consonant Blend**

The combination of two or more consonant sounds without intervening vowel sounds. Each consonant sound retains its original identity. This is in contrast to the consonant digraph. Examples of consonant blends: blend, strap, plow. Some authors and publishers refer to them as *consonant clusters*.

**Consonant Clusters**

See Consonant Blend.

**Consonant Digraph**

Two consonants which are pronounced as a single sound. The individual consonants usually lose their original, single-sound identities. Examples of digraphs: thumb, chin, shoe, wheel, phone.

**Context Reading**

The use of pictures, objects, other words, or meaningful surroundings of any kind to provide clues for reading meaningfully.

**Critical Thinking**

Recognizing and understanding different sides of a written or spoken topic.

**Decode**

Unlocking, or ''taking apart'', the pronunciation of a given word by using the letter-sounds, syllables, and other word-parts (opposite of ''encode'').

**Diacritical Marks**

The markings suggested in the pronunciation key of a dictionary or glossary which serve as the code for pronouncing words. Examples of diacritical marks: FA' vor, kär (car), kãr (care), fôr (four or for).

**Diagnostic Test**

A test designed to locate specific strengths and needs.

**Digraph**

Two successive letters which are pronounced as a single unit. Vowel Digraph: cheat, boat, . . . Consonant Digraph: thumb, chin, shoe, wheel, phone.

**Diphthong**

Two vowels which are combined to form a single blended sound. Example: saw, boot, cow. Also referred to as ''glided vowels'' and ''variant vowels.''

**Dyslexia**

Language-reading disorder in which the ability to read, write, and/or spell are severely impaired.

**Encode**

Forming, or ''putting together'', a word by applying one's knowledge of letter-sounds, syllables, and other word parts (opposite of ''decode'').

**Experience Approach**

See Language Experience Approach.

**Frustration Reading Level**

Reading material at this level is usually too difficult for successful word recognition and understanding. Authors differ in the percentage of words a student can read and questions one can answer which designate frustration, so careful observation for signs of frustration are essential.

**Glided Vowel**
See Diphthong.

**Independent Reading Level**
The level at which a child can read without much direct supervision. Authors differ in the percentage of words a student can read and questions one can answer which designates independence in reading. You will need to observe the student reading various types of materials to help determine the best level and type of material for reading independently.

**Inferential Comprehension**
Understanding what an author says, then thinking beyond the printed word in order to grasp ideas that may be assumed but not specifically stated.

**Instructional Reading Level**
This material is at a level which is most appropriate for instruction. Materials will be somewhat more difficult than those the child can read independently, yet easier than those which cause frustration.

**Language Experience Approach**
A reading approach in which the stories are created by individuals who base the story content on their own experiences.

**Linguistics**
The scientific study of language.

**Listening Level**
The level at which children can comprehend most of the material read to them.

**Literal Comprehension**
Remembering exact details from a story.

**Long Vowels**
The sounds produced by the vowels when we say: $\bar{a}$corn, $\bar{e}$agle, $\bar{i}$ce, $\bar{o}$pen, $\bar{u}$nited.

**Morphology**
The science of the way words are formed.

**Phonics or Phonetic Analysis**
The process of pronouncing letters and groups of letters to determine how a word is pronounced.

**Phonology**
The study of the application of speech sounds in words.

**Prefix**
An addition at the beginning of a word. Example: <u>re</u>write.

**Reading**

The process of understanding information that has been gained through the printed word.

**Root Word**

A basic word to which prefixes (beginnings) and suffixes (endings) can be added. Example: read, (reread), (reading).

**Schwa**

See Variant Vowels.

**Semantics**

The study of the meaning of words.

**Short Vowels**

The sounds produced by the vowels when we say the following: apple, elementary, Indian, octopus, umbrella.

**Sight Words**

Words recognized "at sight", from memory, or by their shape. Words which are not necessarily taught through the blending of letter-sounds. These have also been called "high-frequency words".

**Structural Analysis**

A technique in which the reader identifies meaningful units or word-parts rather than sound elements within words, i.e., roots, suffixes, prefixes, syllables. The reader then relates the word-parts to the total word.

**Suffix**

An addition at the end of the word. Example: reader.

**Variant Vowels**

Vowels that are neither long nor short. These include the diphthongs or glided vowels, plus others: car, air, (r - controlled vowels); mōōn, bŏŏk, (long and short double-vowels); lemon, pencil (*schwa* sounds). The *schwa* is the "uh" sound which can be produced by any of the five major vowels in an unaccented syllable. (The "schwa" is usually represented by the upside-down "e" in the pronunciation key of a dictionary.)

**Visual Discrimination**

The ability to see the similarities and differences between objects, pictures, and visual symbols (letters, words).

**Vowels**

The letters *a, e, i, o* and *u* which produce the major sound unit necessary to form a word. The letter y is a vowel when it represents the sound of a vowel as in try (long i), gym (short i), or happy (long e). The letter w may form a vowel sound together with another vowel, but it is never a vowel by itself: cow, saw.

# INDEX


ability to communicate . . . . . . . . . . . . 54
ability to understand . . . . . . . . . . . . . . 54
accent (marks) . . . . . . . . . . . . . . . . . . . 117
accident prone . . . . . . . . . . . . . . . . . . . 82
achievement, behind in reading, . . . . 52
gap in reading, . . . . . . . . . . . . . . . 52
sacrifice, . . . . . . . . . . . . . . . . . . . . 52
act, think before we, . . . . . . . . . . . . . . 41
actions, communicating through, . . . . 53
actions send signals . . . . . . . . . . . . . . . 53
active listeners and watchers . . . . . . . 43
active listening opportunities . . . . . . . 35
active participants in learning . . . . . . 44
activities . . . . . . . . . . . 79, 83, 87, 93, 99, 102, 106, 109
interesting and meaningful, . . . . . 43
large muscle, . . . . . . . . . . . . . . . . . 56
record observations and, . . . . . . . 73
home and school, . . . . . . . . . . . . 111
observations and, . . . . . . . . . . 67, 75
which help most . . . . . . . . . . . . . . 75
*Adult Basic Education* . . . . . . . . . . . . . 61
adulthood (language experience approach) . . . . . . . . . . . . . . . . . . . . . 60
adults, idea (spelling) for, . . . . . . . . . . 95
adults read, your child must see, . . . 79
adults (who need help in reading) . . . 60
Allen, Roach Van, . . . . . . . . . . . . . . . . 60
allergies . . . . . . . . . . . . . . . . . . . . . . . . . 25
allow time (to think) . . . . . . . . . . . 41, 45
Alpha (activity) . . . . . . . . . . . . . . . . . . . 89
alphabet . . . . . . . . . . . . . . . . . . . . . . 75, 85
Alphabet Book (activity) . . . . . . . . . . . 88
analysis, phonetic, . . . . . . . . . . . . . . . 119
structural, . . . . . . . . . . . . . . . . 29, 120
analyzed, (all) words cannot be, . . . . 92
apply "Language Triangle" . . . . . . . . 64
apply letter-sound understanding . . . . 85
applying reading in daily life . . . . . . . 70
approach, letter-sound, . . . . . . . . . . . . 29
appropriate level of material . . . . . . . . 79
ask for help from school . . . . . . . . . . . 79
ask more . . . . . . . . . . . . . . . . . . . . . 38, 45
asking questions . . . . . . . . . . . . . . . . . . 38
associate beginning sound . . . . . . . . . . 87
ideas . . . . . . . . . . . . . . . . . . . . . . . . 42
letter-sounds . . . . . . . . . . . . . . . . . . 87
assurance, positive, . . . . . . . . . . . . . . . 50
attention . . . . . . . . . . . . . . . . . . . . . . . . 12
attention, desire for, . . . . . . . . . . . . . . 49
attention, fails to pay, . . . . . . . . . . . . 101
attention span, short, . . . . . . . . . . . . . . 77
attitude . . . . . . . . . . . . . . . . 26, 28, 69, 77
and behavior . . . . . . . . . . . . . . 25, 28
lacks positive, . . . . . . . . . . . . . . . . 77
auditory discrimination . . . . . . . . . . . 117
avoid writing and drawing, some children, . . . . . . . . . . . . . . . . . . . . . . . 56
avoidance, signs of, . . . . . . . . . . . . . . 77

*Babies Need Books* . . . . . . . . . . . . . 113
baby understands . . . . . . . . . . . . . . . . . 54
background, educational, . . . . . . . . . . 27
barriers, physical, . . . . . . . . . . . . . . . . . 25
basal reader . . . . . . . . . . . . . . . . . . . . . 117
beginning sound, associate, . . . . . . . . 87
behavior . . . . . . . . . . . . . . . 25, 28, 68, 77
managing the, . . . . . . . . . . . . . . . . 26
behind in reading . . . . . . . . . . . . . . 13, 52
behind, sign of falling, . . . . . . . . . . . . 51
below grade level . . . . . . . . . . . . . . . . . 49
between the line, difficulty reading, 101
writing, . . . . . . . . . . . . . . . . . . . . . . 58
Bingo . . . . . . . . . . . . . . . . . . . . . . . . . . . 89
Bingo, Vocabulary (activity) . . . . . . . 100
blend, consonant, . . . . . . . . . . . . . . . . . 91
blend letter-sounds, cannot, . . . . . . . . 91
blending letter-sounds . . . . . . . . . . . . . 87
blending, left to right, . . . . . . . . . . . . . 94
Book, Alphabet, . . . . . . . . . . . . . . . . . . 88
book clubs . . . . . . . . . . . . . . . . . . . . . . 113
books . . . . . . . . . . . 18-20, 22, 26, 99, 113
for children . . . . . . . . . . . . . . . . . . 113
handling, . . . . . . . . . . . . . . . . . . . . . 19
on idioms, figures of speech, similies . . . . . . . . . . . . . . 100
records and tapes go with . . . . . 107
with cardboard and cloth pages . 20
breakdown in reading . . . . . . . . . . . . . 51
brochures for parents . . . . . . . . . . . . . 114
*Bucket Aids* . . . . . . . . . . . . . . . . . . . . . 116

capital, matching lower-case to, . . . . 89
capitals (letters) . . . . . . . . . . . . . . . 86, 88
cardboard-page books . . . . . . . . . . . . . 20
categorization . . . . . . . . . . . . . . . . . . . . 99
chalkboard, copying from, . . . . . . . . . 59
charts, key word, . . . . . . . . . . . . . . . . . 95
letter, . . . . . . . . . . . . . . . . . . . . . . . . 58
check hearing . . . . . . . . . . . . . . . . . . . . 80
check vision . . . . . . . . . . . . . . . . . . 59, 80

# INDEX


check vision .................. 59, 80
Children's Book
  Council ...................... 114
*Chocolate Moose for Dinner* ..... 100
*Choosing Books for Children* ..... 113
close-range, copying, ..... 59, 108, 109
cloth-pages, non-toxic, ............ 20
clothes pins (as handles on pages) .. 20
clues, punctuation, ............... 104
coloring .......................... 56
coloring book ..................... 57
communicate 31, 45, 47, 52, 55, 61, 64, 70
    creative ideas ................. 55
communicating . 2, 3, 45, 47, 52, 61, 64
communication ............ 45, 61, 111
    between home and school .. 70, 79
    guidelines for, ............. 67, 70
    improve, ..................... 70
    no, .......................... 27
    open, keep, .............. 71, 111
    open the door of, ............ 71
complete sentences ................ 98
complete tasks, does not, ....... 78, 81
completing work ........ 69, 78, 81, 83
comprehension ....... 69, 75, 101-103, 117, 119
    greatest aid to, .............. 102
concentrating, difficulty, ....... 82, 105
concentration (activity) ......... 89, 93
configuration ................. 29, 117
consonant(s) .................. 88, 117
    blend ..................... 91, 117
    clusters ..................... 117
    digraphs ................. 91, 118
context ....... 19, 28-31, 69, 85, 93, 95
    does not use, .............. 92, 98
    clues, improve use of, ......... 93
    of a sentence .............. 28, 29
    reading ...................... 118
conversation ............ 49, 50, 51, 54
copying ....................... 59, 86
    close-range .......... 59, 108, 109
    difficulty, .................. 108
    from a distance ...... 59, 108, 109
correct forms of letters ........ 90, 109
correct pronunciation ............. 50
create stories .................... 60
created, how stories are, ........... 24
creation of pictures and stories ..... 61
creative, child can be, ............. 56
    efforts ...................... 55
    ideas ............. 55, 61, 64, 108
    ways to help .................. 15
creativity ........................ 64
    encourage, ................... 60
    goal of, ...................... 55
creativity
    ultimate goal, ...... 55, 60, 61, 110
    wealth of, .................... 60
Criscuolo, Nicholas, .............. 113
critical thinking ................. 118
cursive (writing) ................. 108
cutting ..................... 108, 109
crying ........................... 49

daily life, apply reading in, ......... 70
decisions, problems making, ....... 81
decode ..................... 92, 118
decreasing (T.V.) viewing time ...... 43
deeper into reading ................ 27
defining words .................... 97
depend on being told .............. 39
depend on someone (to understand) . 2, 35, 37, 45
depend on you at first ............. 53
depend too much ........... 37, 39, 45
details in story ............. 101, 103
determine strengths and needs in
    reading ...................... 77
development, speech, ............. 49
diacritical marks ................. 118
diagnostic testing ................ 118
diary, keep a, .................... 100
Dictionary Spelling (activity) 90, 95, 96
difficulties, learning, ............... 37
difficulties, vision, ................ 25
difficulty
    concentrating ................ 105
    copying ...................... 108
    defining and describing words .. 97
    following directions ........... 82
    forming letters ............... 108
    hopping, skipping, jumping .... 108
    identifying left and right ....... 86
    inferring ..................... 101
    organizing ideas .............. 101
    predicting .................... 101
    reading between the lines ..... 101
    sorting into logical order ....... 82
    varying pattern of sentences .... 97
digraphs ................. 13, 91, 118
diphthong ....................... 118

# INDEX


directions, difficulty following, ..... 82
discrimination ............... 117, 120
distance, copying from, ...... 108, 109
distance, seeing at a, ............. 59
"distant-copying" ................ 59
do, what we, .................. 2, 53
does not
    concentrate .................. 82
    complete tasks ............... 82
    make progress ................ 69
    pace well .................... 82
    recognize sound represented
    by letter .................... 85
    remember how to make letters . 86
    talk or write in complete
        sentences ................ 98
    use context ........... 91, 98, 101
desire, lacks, .................... 76
draw(ing) ........ 23, 24, 52-57, 60, 61,
                        70, 75, 108, 109
drill on reading .................. 26
drilling of reading skills, not a, ..... 26
Durr, William, .................. 115
dyslexia ........................ 118

ear problems ..................... 25
early attempts to write ............ 58
early start in reading ............. 10
Educational Background ........ 25, 27
educational supply stores ...... 95, 116
emphasize strong areas ............ 70
encode ......................... 118
encounters, first (with words) ...... 17
encourage child ............... 79, 84
encourage children to share ........ 64
encourage creativity .............. 60
encouraged to speak ............... 51
encyclopedia ..................... 15
enjoy (new experiences ..... 43, 45, 63
enjoyable, make reading, ...... 17, 23,
                        67, 75, 111
enjoyment of reading, sacrificing, .. 111
environment, home, ..... 25, 26, 28, 51
Ervin, Jane, .................... 113
examination, physical, ............ 80
exciting, make learning, ........... 80
exercise small muscles ............ 56
expectations reasonable
  and clear, make, ................ 83
experience approach ... 24, 60, 80, 118
experience, greatest aid to
  comprehension, ................ 102
    guided, ...................... 44
    in handling books ............ 20
    language ................... 1, 51
experiences, listening ............. 52
experiences
    meaningful, .................. 45
    positive, .................... 56
express creative ideas ............ 64
expressing our needs ........... 47, 61

fails to do tasks ................. 37
fails to meaningfully use words ..... 61
fails to
    pay attention ............... 101
    use context and/or memory .... 91
fall behind in reading ............. 52
feel letters ...................... 89
feelings in words, express, ........ 100
feels, hears, writes (words) ........ 93
figure out meaning ...... 35, 37, 41, 45
figures of speech ................ 100
"fine" muscles ................... 56
fluid build-up in ear .............. 25
following directions, difficulty, ..... 82
forgetful ..................... 37, 45
forgetfulness ..................... 37
form of letter, correct, .... 90, 108, 109
form letters and words ......... 58, 60
form sentences ................... 28
form words ............. 50, 58, 60, 87
forming letters incorrectly .......... 60
forming sounds ................ 49, 50
frustrated with "distance-copying" . 59
frustrated with reading ............ 25
frustration ............. 26, 27, 42, 52
    reading level ................ 118
    signs of, ................. 70, 78
further information and ideas . 112, 113
future reading success ............ 51

gaining information .......... 2, 3, 5, 9
                        10, 31, 52, 63
gap in reading achievement ........ 52
get involved ............. 45, 63, 2, 23
getting involved .............. 33, 43
glided vowel .................... 119
glossary .................... 117-120
goal-creativity, ultimate ........... 55
goal of creativity ................. 55

# INDEX


goals, change . . . . . 71
 limit, . . . . . 109
 major, . . . . . 30
 set, . . . . . 26, 70, 77, 80, 84
golden, silence is, . . . . . 51
good example, set, . . . . . 84
good listener . . . . . 47
good memory . . . . . 13, 37
grade level, below, . . . . . 51
grammar, incorrect, . . . . . 51
greatest aid to comprehension . . . . . 102
greatest need, areas of, . . . . . 70
guesses . . . . . 70
guidance . . . . . 28, 37, 55, 60, 61, 84
 creating with, . . . . . 60
guide . . . . . 44, 45
 someone to, . . . . . 36
guided experience . . . . . 44
 how can child be, . . . . . 37
 involvement . . . . . 44
guidelines . . . . . 30, 67, 69-71, 75, 111
 for communication . . . . . 67, 68
 observation, . . . . . 3, 70
guiding our children . . . . . 63
guiding to touch . . . . . 44
Gwynne, Fred, . . . . . 100

handling books . . . . . 19
Haught, Judy, . . . . . 109
hear and imitate . . . . . 51
hear, do more than see and, . . . . . 43
 feel, see . . . . . 93
 incorrect pronunciation . . . . . 51
hearing
 and understanding language 9, 10, 63
 and using (correct) language . 3, 50
 check, . . . . . 80
 problem . . . . . 50, 82
 screening . . . . . 14, 25
 testing . . . . . 14, 25
help
 child develop responsibilities . . . 84
 from school . . . . . 80
 guide, on how task is organized 84
 understand . . . . . 36
high-frequency words . . . . . 29
high school student . . . . . 51
highs and lows in speech . . . . . 51
Hillerich, Robert, . . . . . 115
hinder success . . . . . 26
holds pencil awkwardly . . . . . 108
home and school, communication
 between, . . . . . 68, 79, 111
home and social environment 25, 26, 28
home environment . . . . . 51
home, reading around, . . . . . 22, 26
"hot," meaning of, . . . . . 41

"I Can Read" box . . . . . 23
idea, main, . . . . . 103
ideas, creative, . . . . . 55, 61, 64, 108
ideas, difficulty organizing, . . . . . 101
ideas, using own (writing), . . . . . 60
identifying left and right . . . . . 86
identifying strengths and needs in
 reading . . . . . 3
idioms . . . . . 100
imitate, sounds to hear and, . . . . . 51
imitate speech . . . . . 49
imitating (writing) . . . . . 58
improve communication . . . . . 68
improve reading . . . . . 17, 26, 67
improve use of context clues . . . . . 93
improvement, what is needed for, . . 111
inactive (children) . . . . . 43
incentive . . . . . 70, 77, 80
incorrect grammar . . . . . 51
incorrect pronunciation . . . . . 50
incorrectly, forming letters, . . . . . 60
independent reading level . . . . . 119
independently, think more, . . . . . 37
inferential comprehension . . . . . 119
inferring, difficulty, . . . . . 101
inflections . . . . . 51
influence learning . . . . . 25, 28
influence reading . . . . . 27
influenced by television . . . . . 27
Influences on Learning to Read 70, 75-80
Influences on Reading Success . . 25, 27
influencing success . . . . . 25
information for parents, further, 113-116
instructional reading level . . . . . 119
intellectually, maturing, . . . . . 29
interesting, make learning, . . . . . 23, 80
interesting to infants, objects, . . . . . 53
International Reading Association . . 114
*Introduction To A Language Experience Program* . . . . . 61
involved, getting, . . . . 22, 33, 42, 45, 63
involved, keep child, . . . . . 23, 111
 parent, teacher, and child should
 be, . . . . . 70

# INDEX


involvement, guided, . . . . . . . . . . . . . . 44
isolated, reading cannot be, . . . . . . . . 67

keep a diary . . . . . . . . . . . . . . . . . . . . 100
keep child involved . . . . . . . . . . . . . . 111
keep communicating . . . . . . . 71, 79, 111
keep record of child's progress . . 67, 73
key word charts . . . . . . . . . . . . . . . . . 95
key words . . . . . . . . . . . . . . . . . . . . . . 87
keys to reading success 17, 27, 31, 63, 68
knowing how to write . . . . . . . . . . . . 59
knowing what learning has occurred 47
knowledge of letter-sounds . . . . . . . . . 29

lacks desire or purpose . . . . . . . . . . . . 78
lacks positive attitude . . . . . . . . . . . . . 77
language areas (categories),
  reading and, . . . . . . . . . 67, 69, 75, 111
language development . . . . . 1, 3, 10, 25
language environment . . . . . . . . . . . . . 11
language, experience, . . . . . . . . . . . . 1,51
language experience approach (to
  reading) . . . . 24, 60, 88, 107, 110, 119
*Language Experience Approach To
  Teaching Reading, The* . . . . . . . . . 61
language experiences . . . . . . . . 3, 53, 67
language growth, breakdown in, . . . . 58
language, hearing and using correct, 51
language need . . . . . . . . . . . . . . . . 52, 57
language, opportunities to use, . . . . . 51
language, reading related to, . . . . . 3, 63
Language Triangle . . . . . . . . . 2, 3, 5, 31
  33, 45, 47, 55, 60, 61-64, 67
language, understanding, . 14, 31, 51, 63
lapses, memory, . . . . . . . . . . . . . . . . . 37
larger muscles . . . . . . . . . . . . . . . . . . . 56
Larrick, Nancy, . . . . . . . . . . . . . . . . . 113
learning
  active participants in, . . . . . . . . . . 43
  difficulties (problems) . . . . . . 21, 37
  exciting, interesting, relevant, . . 80
  getting involved when, . . . . . . . . . 33
  influence, . . . . . . . . . . . . . . . . . 25, 28
  names of letters . . . . . . . . . . . . . . . 89
  to form letters . . . . . . . . . . . . . . . . 58
  (to read) without learning
  letter-sounds or names of letters 85
  to speak . . . . . . . . . . . . . . . . . . . . 49
left and right, difficulty identifying . . 86
left-to-right
  blending . . . . . . . . . . . . . . . . . . . . 94
  not going, . . . . . . . . . . . . . . . . . . . 81
  organization . . . . . . . . . . . . . 108, 109
letter-patterns . . . . . . . . . . . . . . . . . . . 29
letters and sounds, difference among, 25
letters and words, difference between, 86
letters, capitals and lower-case, . . . . . 86
  correct forms of, . . . . . . . . . 90, 109
letters
  forming, . . . . . . . . . . 58, 59, 86, 109
  matching upper and lower-case, 89
  names of, . . . . . . . . . . . . . . . . . 86, 89
  represent sounds . . . . . . . . . . 29, 85
  reversed, . . . . . . . . . . . . . . . . . . . . 86
  see, feel, say, . . . . . . . . . . . . . . . . . 88
  upper-case and lower-case, . . . . . 88
letter-sound
  approach . . . . . . . . . . . . . . . . . . . . 29
  pattern . . . . . . . . . . . . . . . . . . . . . . 28
  relationship . . . . . . . . . . . . . . . . . . 29
  remember, . . . . . . . . . . . . . . . . . . . 87
  understanding . . . . . . . . . . 69, 85, 87
letter-sounds . . . . . 13, 14, 28-30, 69, 95
  associate, . . . . . . . . . . . . . . . . . . . 87
  blending, . . . . . . . . . . . . . . . . . . . . 87
  cannot blend, . . . . . . . . . . . . . . . . . 92
  combination, . . . . . . . . . . . 22, 28, 93
  learning (to read) without
    learning, . . . . . . . . . . . . . . . . . . 85
level of material, appropriate, . . . . . . 79
level that allows success . . . . . . . . . . 106
librarian, ask, . . . . . . . . . . . . . . . . . . . 100
library . . . . . . . . . . . . . . . . . . . . . . . . 116
limit amount of work . . . . . . . . . . . . . 83
limit goals . . . . . . . . . . . . . . . . . . . . . 109
linguistics . . . . . . . . . . . . . . . . . . . 29, 119
listen . . . . . . . . . . . . . . . . . . . . . 14, 64, 68
  not willing to, . . . . . . . . . . . . . . . 78
  frustrated when asked to, . . . . . . 25
  opportunity to, . . . . . . . . . . . . . . . 55
  to stories . . . . . . . . . . . 101, 103, 107
listen (to children) . . . . . . . . . . 36, 37, 57
listener, good, . . . . . . . . . . . . . . . . . . . 47
listening . . . . . . . . . . . . . . . . 2, 5, 9-15, 31
  55, 63, 69, 97, 99, 101-103
  active, . . . . . . . . . . . . . . . . . . . . 35, 43
  experiences, . . . . . . . . . . . . . . . . . . . 5
  level . . . . . . . . . . . . . . . . . . . . . . . 119
literal comprehension . . . . . . . . . . . . 119

# INDEX


Littler, Marie .................... 116
log, keep a diary or, ............. 100
Log, The Reading, ...... 67, 68-72, 111
long vowels .................. 92, 119
looks too quickly at words ......... 91
loses place ...................... 105
losing things ...................... 81
lower-case letters ............... 86-90

main idea ........................ 103
make learning exciting, interesting,
relevant ........................ 80
make expectations reasonable and
clear ............................ 83
make reading comfortable ..... 75, 111
make predictions ................. 103
making decisions, problems, ....... 81
managing the behavior ............. 26
manipulate scissors, cannot, ....... 108
manuscript (printing) ............. 108
Martin, Ruby, .................... 116
matching capital and lower-case
letters .......................... 89
matching sounds .................. 89
material, appropriate level, ......... 79
maturing intellectually ............ 29
McKee, Paul, .................... 115
meaning ...................... 22, 33
meaning of story lost ............ 101
meaning, word, 14, 28, 30, 69, 75, 97-100
meaningful
activities ..................... 43
experience .................... 44
key words ..................... 87
make reading, ......... 23, 75, 111
surroundings (for words) 19, 28, 91
words ................. 30, 61, 87
meaningless, say sounds which are, . 63
mechanics of reading out loud and
silently ......................... 69
memories, capture, ................ 23
memorize words .................. 85
memorized, words that cannot be, .. 29
memorizing .................. 22, 28
memory ......... 13, 17, 28-33, 36, 37,
45, 69, 84, 85
fails to use, ................... 92
poor, .................... 37, 101
visual, ....................... 89
messy papers, desks, drawers ... 81, 83
model, some need a, .............. 57
morphology ..................... 119
moves lips as one reads silently 105, 107
music .................... 12, 88, 106
muscles, small (fine) ............... 56
muscles, larger ................... 56

name of letters ................ 87-90
National Council of
Teachers of English ............ 115
need, language, ................... 51
need, signs of strengths or, ......... 69
needs to be active (children) ....... 43
need time, (children) ........... 42, 56
needs (in reading) 30, 52, 70, 75, 77, 111
needs, expressing our, ......... 47, 61
needs, satisfying our, .............. 43
negative attitude .................. 26
never assume learning has occurred . 64
never too late to learn .............. 3
never underestimate a young child .. 54
Newman, Anabel, ............. 60, 61
newspaper ................ 18, 26, 113
no meaning, words have, .......... 61
nonsense word .................... 30
not interested (in writing and drawing) 56
not taking time to "see" word ...... 91
not willing to listen ............... 78
nothing succeeds like success ...... 71
nurse, school, .................... 80
nursery rhymes ................ 12, 88
nursery school .................... 10

observation guidelines ........... 3, 70
observations ............. (see pg. 75)
attitude and behavior, ......... 25
record, ................... 72, 73
significant, .................. 75
observe your child ................ 30
observed closely, child needs to be, . 52
offer a little experience at a time .... 56
on our own, figure out meaning, 35, 37, 45
on our own, thinking, ... 33, 37, 43, 45
"On Your Own" (writing) .......... 59
open the door of communication .... 70
opinion, reluctant to express, ...... 101
opportunities, active listening, ...... 35
opportunities
to do more than see and hear ... 43
to express creative ideas ....... 61
to express, through actions ..... 55
to speak .................. 52, 61

# INDEX


to think . . . . . . . . . . . . . . . . . . . . . 39
to touch . . . . . . . . . . . . . . . . . . . . . 44
to use different tones . . . . . . . . . . 51
to use language . . . . . . . . . . . . . . . 52
to communicate (drawing) . . . . . . 55
to listen, read, understand, and
think . . . . . . . . . . . . . . . . . . . . . 55
to use words and ideas . . . . . . . . 55
oral reading . . . . . . . . . . . 69, 75, 104-107
organization . . . . . . . . . 42, 69, 75, 81-84
organization, left-to-right, . . . . . 108, 109
organize, a place to, . . . . . . . . . . . . . . . 84
organized, show how task is, . . . . . . . 84
organizing ideas to retell story . . . . . 101
out-loud, reading (also
see oral reading), . . . . . . . . 69, 90, 103

pace well, does not, . . . . . . . . . . . . . . . 82
pamphlets for parents . . . . . . . . . . . . 115
"Parent Activities" . . . . . . . . . . . . . . 113
(also see "activities")
parent, anxiety of any . . . . . . . . . . . . . 55
*Parents and Reading* . . . . . . . . . . . . 115
*Parent's Choice* . . . . . . . . . . . . . . . . 116
*Parent's Guide to Children's
Reading* . . . . . . . . . . . . . . . . . . . . . 113
participants in learning . . . . . . . . . . . 44
participate, actively . . . . . . . . . . . . 43, 45
a child needs to, . . . . . . . . . . . 11, 12
in interesting activities . . . . . 43, 45
participating in listening
experiences . . . . . . . . . . . . . . . . . . . 52
participating in reading
experiences . . . . . . . . . . . . . . . . 22, 52
pattern
in observations . . . . . . . . . . . . . . . 70
of growth in reading . . . . . . . . . . . 73
letter-sound, . . . . . . . . . . . . . . . . . . 28
of strengths and needs . . . . . . . . 111
patterns, letter . . . . . . . . . . . . . . . . . . . 29
vowel, . . . . . . . . . . . . . . . . . . . . . . . 92
pay attention, fails to, . . . . . . . . . . . . 101
phonics . . . . . . . . . . . . . . . . . . . . . . 14, 29
rules . . . . . . . . . . . . . . . . . . . . . 92, 95
physical
barriers . . . . . . . . . . . . . . . . . . . . . . 25
characteristics . . . . . . . . . . . . . 25, 28
examination . . . . . . . . . . . . . . . 25, 80
factors . . . . . . . . . . . . . . . . . . . . . . . 80
pictures as clues (for words) . . . . . . . 28
pictures, creation of, . . . . . . . . . . . . . . 61
plan, write out, . . . . . . . . . . . . . . . . . . . 83
plans, alter, . . . . . . . . . . . . . . . . . . . . . . 71
planned, restructure what is, . . . . . . . 78
planning . . . . . . . . . . . . . . . . . . . 69, 81-84
poems . . . . . . . . . . . . . . . . . . . 13, 88, 106
pointing to each word . . . . . . . . 105, 107
poor memory . . . . . . . . . . . . . . . . . 37, 101
positive assurance . . . . . . . . . . . . . . . . 50
positive attitude, lacks, . . . . . . . . . . . . 77
positive, be . . . . . . . . . . . . . . . . . . . . . . 71
make the experience, . . . . . . . . . . 56
positively respond . . . . . . . . . . . . . . . . 61
practical ideas . . . . . . . . . . . . . . . . . . . . 3
practical information . . . . . . . . . . . . . 67
practice
sounds . . . . . . . . . . . . . . . . . . . . . . . 51
speaking . . . . . . . . . . . . . . . . . . . . . 52
what is learned . . . . . . . . . . . . . . . 27
writing . . . . . . . . . . . . . . . . . . . . . . 60
practicing, don't resist, . . . . . . . . . . . . 17
praise . . . . . . . . . . . . . . . . . . . . 44, 54, 56
your child . . . . . . . . . . . . . . . . . 39, 84
praised . . . . . . . . . . . . . . . . . . . . . . 38, 60
predicting, difficulty, . . . . . . . . . . . . . 101
predictions, make, . . . . . . . . . . . . . . . 103
prefixes . . . . . . . . . . . . . . . . . . . . . . 29, 92
pre-read . . . . . . . . . . . . . . . . . . . . . . . . 103
problem, hearing, . . . . . . . . . . . . . . 50, 82
problem, visual-motor, . . . . . . . . . . . . 82
problem with vision . . . . . . . . . . 107, 109
problems, behavior, . . . . . . . . . . . . . . . 77
problems making decisions . . . . . . . . . 81
progress, child's, . . . . . . . . . . . . . . . . . 69
doesn't make, . . . . . . . . . . . . . . . . . 68
record of, . . . . . . . . . . . . . . . . . . . . 67
student's reading, . . . . . . . . . . . . . 28
pronounce words correctly . . . . . . . . . 61
pronounced properly, hear words, . . 50
psychologist . . . . . . . . . . . . . . . . . . . . . 80
punctuation clues, does not use, . . . 104
PURE reading 17, 18, 27, 30, 31, 63, 68
purpose . . . . . . 17, 18, 27, 30, 31, 63, 68
Pushaw, David, . . . . . . . . . . . . . . . 49, 52
puts in own words
(when reading) . . . . . . . . . . . . . . . . 101

question . . . . . . . . . . . . . . . . . . . . . 42, 50
question your child . . . . . . . . . . . . . . 103
questioning . . . . . . . . . . . . . . . . . . . 39, 84

# INDEX


questioning rather than telling ...... 84
questioning, style of, .............. 39
questions, asking, ................. 38
*Questions Parents Ask About Reading* ...................... 113
quickly at word, looks too, .......... 91
quickly, works too, ............... 82

read .......... 64, 68, 101-103, 104-107
a list ......................... 30
attempting to, ................ 28
meaning to help, .............. 93
silently, ...................... 26
something that is too difficult ... 26
stories ....................... 28
the need to, .................. 18
to your children ........... 26, 27
your child must see adults, ..... 79
*Read-Aloud Handbook, The* ...... 116
reader, basal .................... 117
excellent, .................... 47
successful, ................... 52
readers, reluctant, ................ 103
well-rounded, ................. 22
reading .............. 5, 10, 17, 24-26
55, 60, 63, 69, 97, 99, 120
achievement ............. 13, 52
adults who need help in, ....... 60
aloud ..................... 18, 26
and language areas .......... 2, 3,
67, 69, 75, 111
areas ........................ 28
at a level that allows success .. 106
at home ...................... 26
between the lines, difficulty, .. 101
breakdown in, ................ 51
cannot be isolated ....... 1, 10, 67
comfortable, meaningful, enjoyable, .................. 75
deeper into, .................. 27
development .............. 31, 51
difficulty .................... 25
drill on, ...................... 26
early start in, ................. 10
enjoyment of, .............. 3, 20
excited about, ............. 22, 27
first steps toward, ......... 18, 19
frustration ............... 25
identifying strengths and needs in, 3
improve in, .................. 10
in daily life .................. 70
introduce, ..................... 21
introduced naturally to, ......... 24
language experience approach to, ............ 24, 60
levels ........................ 119
listening and, ............... 2, 31
log ............. 67-69, 72, 73, 111
oral/silent, ........ 69, 75, 104-107
reading
out loud ............. 69, 101, 104
pattern of growth in, .......... 73
preparations for, ............... 9
progress ..................... 28
PURE, ... 17, 18, 27, 30, 31, 63, 68
related to language .... 1, 3, 25, 63
sacrificing enjoyment of, .. 75, 111
silently first ................. 103
specialist ...................... 80
strengths and needs ........... 75
success 17, 22, 24, 27, 30, 31, 51, 55
success, keys to, .......... 63, 68
successful, ................ 17, 67
time-out for, .................. 26
tired when, ................... 25
to your child .............. 21, 99
Triangle .................. 64-67
workbook .................... 13
ready to improve, willing and (writing) ....................... 59
ready to read ................. 10, 35
reasonable and clear, make expectations, ................... 83
reasonable time limit for working ... 80
recall ..... 17, 18, 28, 30, 31, 42, 63, 68
recall sound, does not, ............ 85
recall story-content, can't, ........ 101
recalled from memory, writing errors more frequent when, ............ 85
recalling words, trouble, ........... 97
record of child's progress, ...... 67, 73
record players .................... 13
records ..................... 12, 107
refusing to complete an assignment . 25
relationship between letters, words, and, ................ 88
relevant, make learning, ........... 80
words which are, ............. 99
reluctant readers ................. 103
reluctant to express opinion ....... 101

# INDEX


remember ........ 3, 10, 12, 43, 45, 63
(also see recall)
harder to, .................... 28
more words .................. 50
things, notes to, .............. 84
time to, ...................... 41
remembered, say what is to be, ..... 59
remembering what you see ......... 59
remembering names of letters ...... 85
remembers words ................. 13
repeat familiar vocabulary ......... 97
repeat sounds (babies) ............. 50
repeat words .................... 104
repeating what someone has read ... 28
respond, positively, ............... 61
responsibilities, develop, ........... 84
responsibility, most important, ..... 75
reversals .................. 69, 86, 90
rhyming lines ..................... 88
rhythm, words have, ........... 12, 88
root word ....................... 120
Rule of Thumb .................. 106

say what is to be remembered ...... 59
say words correctly ........... 17, 50
school, apply what is learned in, .... 27
-age children ............. 67, 111
ask for help from, ............. 80
children (writing) in, ........... 58
communication between
home and, .......... 68, 79, 111
nurse ........................ 80
poor attendance at, ............ 78
supplement what is done at, .... 71
schwa .......................... 120
scramble and unscramble sentences . 93
scribble .......................... 56
Schurgin, Audrey, ............... 116
scissors, cannot manipulate, ....... 108
screening, vision and hearing ....... 25
secondary students ................ 75
see and hear, do more than, ........ 43
see, remembering what you, ....... 59
seeing at a distance ............... 59
selective in what to watch (television) 27
semantics ...................... 120
send signals, actions, .............. 53
sentence, differences between word
and, ........................... 86
strips ....................... 23
sentences ........................ 51
complete, .................... 98
context of, ................... 28
form, ........................ 28
relationship between letters, words,
and, ........................ 88
run together ................. 104
scramble and unscramble, ...... 93
short, ................ 11, 13, 51
writing, ...................... 14
set a goal ....................... 26
set goals .................. 70, 80, 84
set good example .... 18, 21, 26, 27, 84
severe learning problem ........... 21
sharing time ..................... 26
Sharp, (Florence) Dinghy, ........ 116
social environment ......... 25, 26, 28
short attention span ............... 77
short sentences ............ 11, 13, 51
short stories are essential ......... 103
short vowels ................ 92, 120
show
how letters are formed ......... 60
how pages are turned .......... 21
how task is organized ......... 84
shows interest, infant .............. 53
shows understanding (baby) ........ 54
sight or sound, disturbed by slightest, 82
sight-words ............ 29, 91, 94, 120
sign of falling behind .............. 52
signals
actions send, ........... 25, 30, 53
children send, ................ 53
that show us (what was learned) 27
sending , ..................... 54
watch for, .................... 61
significant observations ............ 75
signs
of avoidance .................. 78
of frustration .............. 70, 78
of learning difficulties ......... 37
of strengths or need ........... 12
silence, philosophy of, ............. 52
silent reading ......... 69, 75, 105, 107
silently read .................. 26, 103
similies ......................... 100
sing ............................ 12
skill, don't stress specific, ..... 75, 111
"small" letters ................... 88
small muscles ..................... 56

# INDEX


social environment . . . . . . . . . 25, 26, 28
social worker . . . . . . . . . . . . . . . . . . . . 80
songs . . . . . . . . . . . . . . . . . . . . . . . . . . 12
sound, beginning, . . . . . . . . . . . . . . . . 88
-blending . . . . . . . . . . . . . . . . . . . . 29
disturbed by slightest, . . . . . . . . . 82
does not recall, . . . . . . . . . . . . . . . 85
sounding-out . . . . . . . . . . . . . . . 29, 92, 93
sounds
animal, . . . . . . . . . . . . . . . . . . . . . . 51
and inflections . . . . . . . . . . . . . . . . 51
become words . . . . . . . . . . . . . . . . 50
sounds
communicating through, . . . . . . . 49
important to hear and imitate, . . 51
letters represent, . . . . . . . 29, 85, 87
meaningless, . . . . . . . . . . . . . . . . . . 63
practice, . . . . . . . . . . . . . . . . . . . . . 51
repeat (babies), . . . . . . . . . . . . . . . 50
syllables and, . . . . . . . . . . . . . . . . . 51
vowel, . . . . . . . . . . . . . . . . . . . . . . . 92
speak
encouraged to, . . . . . . . . . . . . . . . . 51
learning to, . . . . . . . . . . . . . . . . . . . 49
now allowed to, . . . . . . . . . . . . . . . 51
opportunities to, . . . . . . . . . . . 51, 61
speaking . . . . . 25, 26, 50, 55, 69, 97, 99
practice in, . . . . . . . . . . . . . . . . . . 52
specialized testing . . . . . . . . . . . . . . . . 14
specific reading difficulty . . . . . . . . . . 25
specific skill, don't stress . . . . . . . . . . 75
speech, imitate . . . . . . . . . . . . . . . . . . 49
and language pathologist
(teacher) . . . . . . . . . . . . 11, 14, 80
development . . . . . . . . . . . . . . . . . . 49
highs and lows in, . . . . . . . . . . . . . 51
spelling . . . . . . . . . . . . . . . . . . . . . . . . . 25
Spelling Dictionary . . . . . . . . . 90, 95, 96
Speed Up, Word (activity) . . . . . . . . . 94
spend time wisely . . . . . . . . . . . . . . . . 70
stages, children draw in, . . . . . . . . 56-59
stages of forming letters and words . 58
standard of silence . . . . . . . . . . . . . . . 52
starts at bottom (when writing) . . 81, 86
Stauffer, Russell, . . . . . . . . . . . . . . 60, 61
stimulate improvement (writing) . 81, 86
stores, educational supply, . . . . . 95, 116
stories
based on experience . . . . . . . . . . . 60
creation of, . . . . . . . . . . . . 23, 60, 61
language experience, . . 23, 107, 110
listen to, . . . . . . . . . . . . . . . . . . . . 103
short, . . . . . . . . . . . . . . . . . . . . . . . 103
share, . . . . . . . . . . . . . . . . . . . . . . . . 26
understanding, . . . . . . . . . . . . . . . . 30
story content, can't recall, . . . . . . . . 101
story, conversation in a, . . . . . . . . . . 106
not understanding, . . . . . . . . . . . 101
retell, . . . . . . . . . . . . . . . . . . . . . . . 101
strengthen small and large muscles . . 56
strengths . . . . . 3, 30, 69, 70, 75, 77, 111
strong areas, emphasize, . . . . . . . . . . . 70
structural analysis . . . . . . . . . . . . 29, 120
student's reading progress . . . . . . . . . 27
style of questioning . . . . . . . . . . . . . . . 39
succeed in reading . . . . . . . . . . . . . . . . 67
succeed in speaking, reading, spelling 25
success, allow
evidence of, . . . . . . . . . . . . . . . . . . 73
hinder, . . . . . . . . . . . . . . . . . . . . . . . 25
influencing, . . . . . . . . . . . . . . . . . . . 25
nothing succeeds like, . . . . . . . . . 71
reading, . . . . . . . . . . . . . . 17, 22, 24,
27, 30, 31, 49, 55, 67
taste (writing and drawing), . . . . 56
successful and enjoyable, reading, . . 67
successful reader . . . . . . . . . . . . . . . . . 52
successful reading . . . . . . . . . . . . . . 3, 25
suffix . . . . . . . . . . . . . . . . . . . . . . . . . 120
suggestions for improvement . . . . . . . 25
support services . . . . . . . . . . . . . . . . 113
symbols represent sounds . . . . . . . . . . 85
syllables . . . . . . . . . . . . 26, 29, 49, 50, 92

take time (to think) . . . . . . . . . . . . . 41-45
taking time to "see" word . . . . . . . . . 91
talk
about (new experiences) . . . . 23, 44
about (T.V.) programs . . . . . . . . . 27
or write in complete sentences,
does not, . . . . . . . . . . . . . . . . . . . 98
reluctant to, . . . . . . . . . . . . . . . . . . 98
with teacher . . . . . . . . . . . . . . . 70, 71
with your child . . . . . . . . . . . 13, 100
talking . . . . . . . . . . . . . . . . . . . . . . . . . 49
talks all the time . . . . . . . . . . . . . . . . . 52
tape recorder, use, . . . . . . . 12, 103, 106
tardiness . . . . . . . . . . . . . . . . . . . . . . . . 78
task, discuss, . . . . . . . . . . . . . . . . . . . . 83
tasks, fails to do, . . . . . . . . . . . . . . 37, 81
taste success (writing and drawing) . 56

# INDEX


*Teach Your Child To Talk* . . . . . . . . . 52
teacher, consult child's, . . . . . . . . . . 106
teacher stores . . . . . . . . . . . . . . . . . . 116
tell less . . . . . . . . . . . . . . . . . . . . . . . . . 38
testing, specialized, . . . . . . . . . . . . . . . 14
testing, vision and hearing . . . . . . . . . 25
television . . . . . . . . . . 19, 26, 27, 43, 99
think . . . . . . . . . . . . . . . . . . . . . . . . . . . 39
allow time to, . . . . . . . . . . . . . 41, 45
before we act . . . . . . . . . . . . . . . . 41
opportunity to, . . . . . . . . . . . 39, 55
take time to, . . . . . . . . . . . . 39-43, 45
time to, . . . . . . . 2, 33, 41-45, 54, 63
thinking . . . . . . . . . . . . . . . . . . 24, 38, 60
critical, . . . . . . . . . . . . . . . . . . . . . 118
deep, . . . . . . . . . . . . . . . . . . . . . . . . 47
on our own, 2, 33, 35, 37, 43, 45, 63
time . . . . . . . . . . . . . . . . . . . . . . . . . 42
Thumb, Rule of, . . . . . . . . . . . . . . . . . 106
time
allowing, . . . . . . . . . . . . . . 41, 45, 54
children need, . . . . . . . . . . . . . . . . 57
and experience, writing grows with, . . . . . . . . . . . . . . . . . . . . . . 57
limit for working, reasonable, . . 80
-out for reading . . . . . . . . . . . . . . . 26
take (to think) . . . . . . . . . . 39, 41-45
to remember and associate . . . . . 42
to think . . . . . . . 2, 33, 41-45, 54, 63
wisely, spend, . . . . . . . . . . . . . . . . 70
tired when reading . . . . . . . . . . . . . . . . 25
"too young to understand" . . . . . . . . 36
"Trace-Over" . . . . . . . . . . . . . . . 59, 109
Trelease, Jim . . . . . . . . . . . . . . . . . . . 116
Truby, Roy . . . . . . . . . . . . . . . . . . . . 115
turns letters and words around . . . . . 86
turn the pages of a book . . . . . . . . 20, 21

ultimate goal-creativity . . . . . . 55, 60, 61
understand . . . . . . . . . . 10, 14, 17, 31, 35, 37, 43-45, 54, 63, 68
help child, . . . . . . . . . . . . . . . . . . . . 11
child's needs, family must, . . . . . 80
too young to, . . . . . . . . . . . . . . . . . 36
understanding . . . . . . . . 2, 3, 14, 17, 18, 27, 30, 31, 44, 45, 54, 60, 63
communicate, . . . . . . . . . . . . . . . . 52
demonstrate, . . . . . . . . . . . . . . 36, 52
letter-sound, . . . . . . . . . . . . 69, 85-89
of language . . . . . . . . . . . . . . . 51, 63
shows, (baby) . . . . . . . . . . . . . 54, 61
spoken language . . . . . . . . . . . . . . 97
stories . . . . . . . . . . . . . . . . . . . . . . . 30
what one reads . . . . . . . . . . . . . . . 69
words . . . . . . . . . . . . . . . . . . . . . . . . 69
understands meaning of new experience . . . . . . . . . . . . . . . . . . . . . 49
understands meanings (of words) . . . 14, 19, 30
understood by others, words *not*, . . . 50
unfamiliar words . . . . . . . . . . . . . . . . . 37
unlocking words . . . . . . . . . . . . . . . 29, 85
unscramble sentences . . . . . . . . . . . . . 93
upper-case letters . . . . . . . . . . . . . . . . 88

variant vowels . . . . . . . . . . . . . . . . . . 120
vision . . . . . . . . . . . . . . . . . . . . . . . . . . 25
check, . . . . . . . . . . . . . . . 59, 80, 107
problems with, . . . . . . . . 25, 81, 108
screening . . . . . . . . . . . . . . . . . . . . 25
visual discrimination . . . . . . . . . . . . . 120
visual memory . . . . . . . . . . . . . . . . . . . 89
visual-motor problem . . . . . . . . . . . . . 21
vocabulary . . . . . . . . . . . . . . . . . . . . . . 30
Vocabulary Bingo (activity) . . . . . . . 103
vocabulary, repeats familiar, . . . . . . . 97
vowels . . . . . . . . . . . . . . . . . . 92, 119, 120

wants own way . . . . . . . . . . . . . . . . . . 78
watch and positively respond . . . . . . . 61
(children) . . . . . . . . . . . . . . 36, 37, 57
do more than, . . . . . . . . . . . . . . . . 45
for signals . . . . . . . . . . . . . . . . . . . . 61
television with our children . . . . 27
your child . . . . . . . . . . . . . . . . . . . . 53
watchers, active, . . . . . . . . . . . . . . . . . 43
wealth of creativity . . . . . . . . . . . . . . . 60
well-rounded readers . . . . . . . . . . . . . 22
whispers and moves lips as one reads silently . . . . . . . . . . . . . . . . . . 105, 107
willing and ready to improve . . . . . . . 59
withdraws . . . . . . . . . . . . . . . . . . . . . . . 77
word and sentence, difference between, . . . . . . . . . . . . . . . . . . . . . . . 86
word-by-word pointing . . . . . . . . . . . . 95
word
add, . . . . . . . . . . . . . . . . . . . . . . . . 104
meaning . . . . . 28, 30, 69, 75, 97-100
parts . . . . . . . . . . . . . . . 28, 29, 69, 92
problem, . . . . . . . . . . . . . . . . . . . . . 94
recognition . . . . . . . . 26, 28, 29, 69, 75, 87, 90, 91-96

# INDEX


word
root, . . . . . . . . . . . . . . . . . . . . . . . . 120
Speed Up (activity) . . . . . . . . . . . 94
trouble recalling, . . . . . . . . . . . . . . 97
words
cannot be analyzed, all, . . . . . . . . 92
cannot be spoken, full, . . . . . . . . 49
confused, . . . . . . . . . . . . . . . . . . . . 93
context clues for, . . . . . . . . . . . . . 91
correctly, say, . . . . . . . . . . . . . . . . 51
difficulty defining, . . . . . . . . . . . . . 97
difficulty thinking of, . . . . . . . . . . 13
distinguishing individual, . . . . . . . 28
feels, hears, writes, . . . . . . . . . . . 93
form, . . . . . . . 29, 50, 51, 58, 59, 87
from memory . . . . . . . . . . . . . . . . . 22
have more than one meaning . . . 98
have no meaning . . . . . . . . . . . . . . 61
have rhythm . . . . . . . . . . . . . . . . . . 88
high-frequency, . . . . . . . . . . . . . . . 29
in a list . . . . . . . . . . . . . . . . . . . . . . 30
key, . . . . . . . . . . . . . . . . . . . . . . . . . 87
learning, . . . . . . . . . . . . . . . . . . . . . 85
meaningful, . . . . . . . . . . . . . . . 30, 31
new, . . . . . . . . . . . . . . . . . . 14, 28, 29
nonsense, . . . . . . . . . . . . . . . . . . . . 30
not saying meaningful, . . . . . . . . . 30
not understood by others . . . . . . 50
omit, . . . . . . . . . . . . . . . . . . . . . . . 104
opportunity to use, . . . . . . . . . . . . 55
pointing to, . . . . . . . . . . . . . . . . . . 105
reading new, . . . . . . . . . . . . . . . . . 42
relevant, . . . . . . . . . . . . . . . . . . . . . 99
remember, . . . . . . . . . . . . . . . . . . . 51
reversed, . . . . . . . . . . . . . . . . . . . . . 86
saying, . . . . . . . . . . . . . . . . . . . . . . . 17
words
sight, . . . . . . . . . . . . . . . . . . . . . . . . 29
sound-out or decode, . . . . . . . . . . 91
sounds become, . . . . . . . . . . . . . . . 50
substitute, . . . . . . . . . . . . . . . . . . . 104
understanding meanings of, . . . . 30
unfamiliar, . . . . . . . . . . . . . . . . . . . 37
unlocking . . . . . . . . . . . . . . . . . 29, 85
work, getting out of hard, . . . . . . . . . . 56
workbook, reading, . . . . . . . . . . . . . . . 13
works best, what, . . . . . . . . . . . . . . . . 71
works too slowly or too quickly . . . . 82
write . . . . . . . . . . . . . . . . . . . 15, 43, 55-60
a report . . . . . . . . . . . . . . . . . . . . . 15
complete sentences . . . . . . . . . . . . 98
letters . . . . . . . . . . . . . . . . . . . . . . . 90
lists, encourage your child to, . . 84
out plan . . . . . . . . . . . . . . . . . . . . . 83
writes, feels, hears, (words) . . . . . . . . 91
writing . . . . . . . . . . . . . 14, 24, 52-60, 97, 99, 108-110
and drawing . . . 60, 69, 75, 108-110
avoid, . . . . . . . . . . . . . . . . . . . . . . . 56
between the lines . . . . . . . . . . . . . 58
does not properly use spaces when, . . . . . . . . . . . . . . . . . . . . . . 81
from memory, errors when, . . . . 86
from wrong side of paper, . 86, 108
lesson . . . . . . . . . . . . . . . . . . . . . . . 60
practice . . . . . . . . . . . . . . . . . . . . . . 60

young child 9, 11, 19, 28, 35, 36, 49, 55
young children . . . . . . 10, 23, 38, 49, 60
*Your Child Can Read And You Can Help* . . . . . . . . . . . . . . . . . . . . . . . . . 113

# About the Author

Linda McCorkel Clinard developed a rich professional background through experience as a classroom teacher and reading specialist. In addition, as a mother, she brings to bear the unique perspective that can only be gained by raising one's own child. From 1964–1978, she taught at the elementary and secondary levels in California, Illinois, New York, Michigan, and overseas for the Department of Defense Schools in Okinawa and Germany. Dr. Clinard received her masters degree in Reading Education from Indiana University, Bloomington, Indiana, and her Ph.D. from the University of Michigan, Ann Arbor. Currently, Dr. Clinard provides consultant and speaking services, and serves as Distinguished Lecturer of graduate reading courses for Michigan State University in Birmingham, Michigan.